CAMPAIGN 398

PORT ARTHUR 1904–05

The First Modern Siege

ROBERT FORCZYK

ILLUSTRATED BY STEVE NOON
Series editor Nikolai Bogdanovic

OSPREY PUBLISHING
Bloomsbury Publishing Plc
Kemp House, Chawley Park, Cumnor Hill, Oxford OX2 9PH, UK
29 Earlsfort Terrace, Dublin 2, Ireland
1385 Broadway, 5th Floor, New York, NY 10018, USA
E-mail: info@ospreypublishing.com
www.ospreypublishing.com

OSPREY is a trademark of Osprey Publishing Ltd

First published in Great Britain in 2024

© Osprey Publishing Ltd, 2024

A catalogue record for this book is available from the British Library.

ISBN: PB 9781472855633; eBook 9781472855602; ePDF 9781472855626;
XML 9781472855619

24 25 26 27 28 10 9 8 7 6 5 4 3 2 1

Maps by Bounford.com
3D BEVs by Paul Kime
Index by Zoe Ross
Typeset by PDQ Digital Media Solutions, Bungay, UK
Printed and bound in India by Replika Press Private Ltd.
Osprey Publishing supports the Woodland Trust, the UK's leading woodland
conservation charity.

To find out more about our authors and books visit
www.ospreypublishing.com. Here you will find extracts, author
interviews, details of forthcoming events and the option to sign up for
our newsletter.

Artist's note

Readers may care to note that the original paintings from which the colour
plates in this book were prepared are available for private sale. All
reproduction copyright whatsoever is retained by the publishers. The artist
can be contacted via the following website:

www.steve-noon.co.uk

The publishers regret that they can enter into no correspondence upon
this matter.

Photographic images

Unless otherwise indicated, the photographs that appear in this work are
public domain.

Note on currency values

The value of the Japanese Yen between 1897 and 1900 was approximately
¥2 = $1 (US) or ¥9.7 = £1 (UK). The value of the Russian ruble was
approximately 1.97 ruble = $1 (US) in 1900.

Abbreviations and acronyms

AP	armour-piercing
CER	China Eastern Railway
HE	high explosive
IJA	Imperial Japanese Army
IJN	Imperial Japanese Navy
QF	quick firing
ROKK	*Rossiyskogo Obshchestva Krasnogo Kresta* (Russian Red Cross)

Rank equivalents

English rank	Russian rank	Japanese rank
General	General	Rikugun-Taisho
Lieutenant-General	General-leytenant	Rikugun-Chujo
Major-General	General-mayor	Rikugun-Shosho
Colonel	Polkovnik	Rikugun-Taisa
Lieutenant-Colonel	Podpolkovnik	Rikugun-Chusa
Major		Rikugun-Shosa
Captain	Kapitan	Rikugun-Tai-i
	Shtabs-kapitan	
Lieutenant	Poruchik	Rikugun-Chui
Second Lieutenant	Podporuchik	Rikugun-Shoi

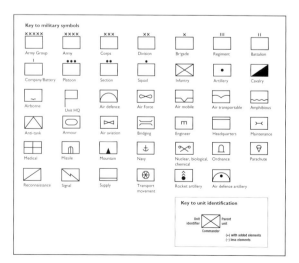

Front cover main illustration: On 23/24 August 1904, Japanese
soldiers from the 7th Regiment – illuminated by searchlights,
magnesium flares and heavy fire – attempt to breach barbed-wire
obstacles erected by the Russian defenders on the eastern side of
the Wantai Heights. (Steve Noon)

Title page image: Japanese wounded troops recovering behind the
lines. (Author's collection)

CONTENTS

The Strategic Situation in Manchuria, 5 May 1904

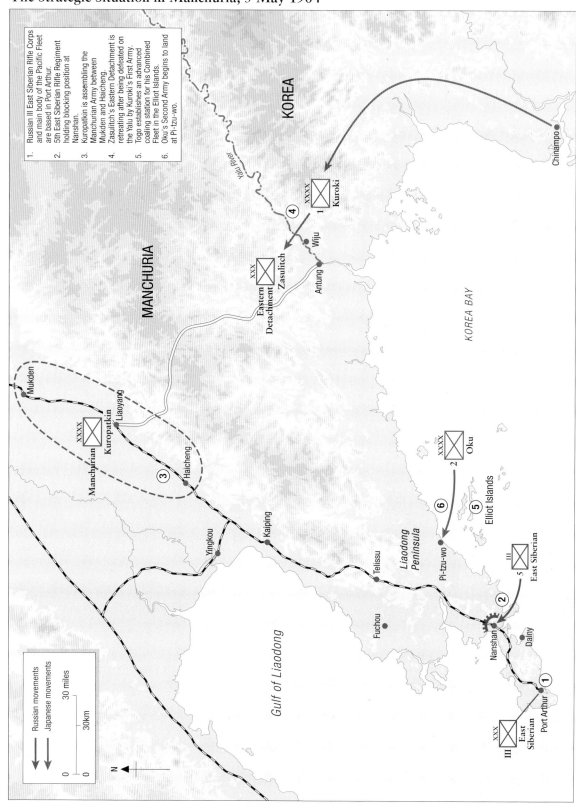

1. Russian III East Siberian Rifle Corps and main body of the Pacific Fleet are based in Port Arthur.
2. 5th East Siberian Rifle Regiment holding blocking position at Nanshan.
3. Kuropatkin is assembling the Manchurian Army between Mukden and Haicheng.
4. Zasulitch's Eastern Detachment is retreating after being defeated on the Yalu by Kuroki's First Army.
5. Togo establishes an advanced coaling station for his Combined Fleet in the Elliot Islands.
6. Oku's Second Army begins to land at Pi-tzu-wo.

KOREA

MANCHURIA

Yalu River

Kuroki
1

Wiju

Antung

Eastern
Detachment
Zasulitch

KOREA BAY

Mukden

Liaoyang

Manchurian
Kuropatkin

Haicheng

Oku
2

Elliot Islands

Yingkou

Kaiping

Liaodong
Peninsula

Pi-tzu-wo

Telissu

III
5
East Siberian

Fuchou

Nanshan

Dalny

Gulf of Liaodong

III
East
Siberian

Port Arthur

Chinampo

Russian movements
Japanese movements

30 miles

30km

0

0

N

ORIGINS OF THE CAMPAIGN

Allegedly, Aristotle stated over two millennia ago that 'nature abhors a vacuum'. Near the end of the 19th century, the hold of the decaying Qing Dynasty over Manchuria in north-east China was becoming quite tenuous – and it invited aggression from various foreign predators. In particular, Tsarist Russia was interested in expanding its sphere of influence in the Far East and Manchuria appeared to be a tempting prize. Russia had already embarked upon building the Trans-Siberian Railway, which would eventually establish a direct connection between European Russia and the Far East. However, Imperial Japan, which was just beginning to embark upon its own expansionist phase, was also interested in the potential resources in Korea and Manchuria. Mutual imperialistic ambitions, in regard to Manchuria and Korea, set Russia and Japan upon a collision course.

Although the Qing Dynasty was in decline, the Empress Dowager Cixi recognized the foreign threat to her control over Manchuria and authorized measures to modernize Chinese military capabilities. The so-called self-strengthening movement led to more resources being devoted towards maritime defence, with new warships being purchased abroad in an effort to discourage foreign encroachments in coastal areas. The most powerful force was the Beiyang Fleet (Northern Seas Fleet), consisting of ten modern, armoured warships. In 1881, the Qing Dynasty chose the heretofore minor fishing port at Lüshunkou (Lüshun) on the southern end of the Liaodong Peninsula to be the site of a new naval facility, intended to be the home port for the Beiyang Fleet. At the time, Lüshunkou had a population of only about 4,000, which was insufficient to provide enough labour for a surge effort in construction. Constantin von Hanneken, a Prussian military engineer, was hired by the Qing Dynasty to design and construct the base. Over the course of the next decade, Lüshunkou was transformed into a small but useful naval facility, with a drydock and coal storage. Von Hanneken also laid out a ring of 22 small forts and coastal batteries to protect the base, which were intended to be equipped with modern Krupp-made artillery pieces. Nevertheless, China's veneer of military modernization was undermined by deep-rooted incompetence and corruption, which was brutally exposed when competition over Korea caused Japan to declare war in August 1894.

Japan's 120,000-man field army in 1894 (six infantry divisions and the Imperial Guard) was only one-quarter the size of the Qing Army, and the Imperial Japanese Navy (IJN) had no battleships, unlike the Beiyang Fleet. Nevertheless, the better-led and better-trained IJN quickly demolished the Beiyang Fleet in the Battle of the Yalu River, and then two small Japanese

Japanese troops allegedly killed large numbers of Chinese military prisoners and civilians when they captured Lüshun in November 1894. The rapid capture of the port in the Sino-Japanese War led the leadership in Tokyo to expect another easy triumph when facing the Russians in 1904. (Author's collection)

armies invaded Manchuria. General Oyama Iwao's Second Army was assigned to isolate and occupy the Liaodong Peninsula. By the time that Oyama's Second Army reached Dalian (Dalny) in October 1894, the Chinese had reinforced the defence of Lüshunkou with 20,000 troops and over 200 artillery pieces. Oyama committed the 1st Infantry Division, the 12th Mixed Brigade and a small artillery train (with limited ammunition) to attack the port, which seemed well short of the numerical superiority recommended for assaulting a fortified position. Despite the odds, the Japanese moved aggressively and began their attack on the night of 20/21 November, which quickly unhinged the Chinese defence. Most of the Qing officers deserted, leaving their leaderless troops to their fate. Major-General Nogi Maresuke, commanding the 1st Infantry Brigade, led the assault, which broke through the Chinese fortified line by noon on 21 November, causing the entire defence to collapse like a house of cards. At a cost of just 288 casualties, the Japanese Army was able to capture Lüshunkou intact in less than a day of fighting. In the immediate aftermath of the city's fall, Japanese troops killed over 2,000 Chinese civilians and troops allegedly dressed as civilians.

Under the terms of the Treaty of Shimonoseki, which ended the Sino-Japanese War on 17 April 1895, the Qing Dynasty ceded the Liaodong Peninsula to Japan. However, Russia was unwilling to see such a plum fall into Japan's lap and used diplomacy to enlist France and Germany into signing a joint *démarche*, dubbed 'the Triple Intervention', demanding that Japan abandon its claim upon the Liaodong Peninsula. In return, Japan was offered a larger war indemnity from China. Implicit within the *démarche* was the threat of Russian military intervention if Japan did not comply; unwilling to risk a fight with a coalition of European powers, the Japanese leadership grudgingly acquiesced to the terms after six months of diplomatic haggling. When the Japanese troops finally left Port Arthur, they destroyed most of the Chinese fortifications and damaged the port facilities. Afterwards, Japan's leaders decided to increase their control over Korea and to invest much of the Chinese indemnity into a new round of military modernization efforts for both the Imperial Army and Navy. The Japanese military budget increased dramatically after the First Sino-Japanese War, rising from ¥20 million ($10 million) in 1895 to ¥73 million ($36.5 million) in 1896, then ¥100 million ($50 million) in 1900. By the turn of the century, Japan was spending half its national budget and 5.8 per cent of its gross domestic product (GDP) on military modernization. The Japanese military used the funds to purchase six battleships from England, double the size of the army to 13 divisions and modernize its artillery and small arms. The insulting coercion of the Triple Intervention also led to an upsurge in Japanese nationalism, which the government harnessed in order to facilitate its own expansionist policies.

Having blocked Japan from acquiring the Liaodong Peninsula, Russia moved quickly to achieve its own interests in Manchuria. The Qing regime was in no position to resist Russian overtures, since it was bankrupt and both its army and navy had been demolished as a result of the Sino-Japanese War. On 3 June 1896, Russia coerced Qing diplomats into signing a secret treaty in Moscow; in return for Russia loaning funds (mostly borrowed from French bankers) to China to help pay its indemnity to Japan, China would grant permission to build a railway across northern Manchuria and to allow Russian warships to use the port of Lüshunkou. A joint stock company was set up to build the China Eastern Railway (CER) in order to give the impression that this was a private venture, not an annexation. However, once construction of the CER began in July 1897, the Russian government decided to abandon the subtle approach, particularly after the German East Asia Squadron coerced Qing officials into providing a 99-year lease on the port of Kiaochow (Qingdao). In December 1897, two weeks after the German coup, a Russian naval squadron under Vice Admiral Yevgeni I. Alekseyev was sent to Lüshunkou, and through a combination of bribes and implied threats, managed to acquire a 25-year lease on the entire Liaodong Peninsula. By March 1898, the Russians had taken full control over Lüshunkou, garrisoned it with the 3rd East Siberian Rifle Brigade and began referring to it by its English name, Port Arthur. In January 1900, the Russian War Ministry approved plans to fortify Port Arthur.

The seizure of Chinese ports by means of 'unequal treaties' and veiled threats incited widespread anti-imperialist agitation across China. Lacking the military resources to oppose the foreign imperialists directly, the Empress Dowager Cixi encouraged anti-foreign protests, which led to the outbreak of the Boxer Rebellion in June 1900. When the Boxers and local Qing troops began conducting attacks against the CER, causing some damage and casualties, Tsar Nicholas II used this as a pretext to order direct Russian military intervention in Manchuria. At the time, the Russian Army had just 23,000 troops in the neighbouring Amur Military District, but it was enough. The Russian troops crushed the Boxers and Qing forces with great brutality, and by 20 September 1900 the Russians were in complete control of Manchuria. Although both the Germans and Japanese also sent large expeditionary forces into northern China in response to the Boxer Rebellion, they did not remain for long.

The Imperial Russian Navy wanted Port Arthur as the primary base for its Pacific Squadron since its existing base at Vladivostok was blocked by ice during winter months. Indeed, the Russian Pacific Squadron (which usually amounted to just a few cruisers) prior to 1895 was little more than a transitory presence, spending its winter months at other ports throughout Asia and its warships could only stay in the region for about a year before having to return to Europe for maintenance. By acquiring a warm-water base like Port Arthur, the Russian Navy could permanently deploy capital ships to the region. Soon

The inner harbour area in Russian-held Port Arthur, c.1901. The rapid build-up of Russian naval capability at this port was one of the proximate causes that led to the Japanese decision to go to war in 1904. (Author's collection)

after acquiring the lease on Port Arthur, two Russian battleships were sent there in 1898 and they remained for three years. Yet Port Arthur was far from ideal as a naval base. The harbour entrance was only 290m wide and could easily be blocked, while the main channel was just 6m deep at low tide. Consequently, battleships could only enter or leave the port at high tide. The large drydock in the port was expanded in order to accommodate the Petropavlovsk-class battleships, but the primitive machine shops in situ could only manage minor repairs. Any substantial repair work would require capital ships to return to the Baltic yards. The amount of skilled labour and material available in Port Arthur was also extremely limited – adequate to support a small squadron but not a battle fleet. The total population of Port Arthur in early 1904 was just 51,000, of which about 15,000 were Russian and European civilians, the rest Chinese. Nevertheless, both Tsar Nicholas II and the Navy leadership were fascinated by the potential of Port Arthur as a future springboard for Russian naval power in the region, and ignored these constraints.

Russia's de facto annexation of Manchuria antagonized the leadership in Tokyo, but Japan still needed time to upgrade and modernize its army and navy before taking on a European power. Sergei Witte, the Tsar's finance minister, recognized that conflict with Japan was increasingly likely and sought to use diplomacy to soothe Japan's wounded pride over the loss of the Liaodong Peninsula. Russia had signed the Nishi-Rosen Agreement in April 1898, which recognized Japanese economic interests in Korea in return for Japan recognizing the Russian sphere of influence in Manchuria. However, Russia did not honour the agreement and repeatedly attempted to promote its own economic interests in Korea, which led to the Masanpo Incident in 1899. Russian policies in the Far East were influenced by the so-called 'Bezobrazov circle', led by the ex-military entrepreneur Aleksandr M. Bezobrazov and included Vice Admiral Alekseyev and other members of the Russian aristocracy. Bezobrazov and his associates aggressively pushed to acquire logging and mining rights in Korea as a prelude to establishing bases, backed up by Russian ground and naval power. In an effort to reduce the risk of war in the Far East, Witte signed an agreement with the Qing Dynasty in April 1902 which asserted that the Russian Army would begin a phased 18-month withdrawal from Manchuria. Witte also assured Japanese diplomats that Russia would honour the Nishi-Rosen Agreement. For a brief moment, a peaceful solution seemed feasible.

However, Nicholas II proved unwilling to make concessions to a country which he perceived to be a second-rate power. Alekseyev and other senior military advisors convinced the Tsar that Japan would back down if Russia adopted an aggressive approach. Amazingly, the Tsar supported Bezobrazov's imperialistic schemes and decided to grant him both state funds and troops to support his activities in Korea. Emboldened by the Tsar's support, Bezobrazov sent Russian troops to the Yalu River in May 1903 (known as the Yongampo Incident) to protect logging operations on Korean soil – which the Japanese regarded as a violation of the Nishi-Rosen Agreement. General Aleksei N. Kuropatkin, as war minister, favoured abandoning southern Manchuria and argued that Bezobrazov's economic interests in Korea were not worth risking war, but the Tsar ignored him. Shortly thereafter, the Tsar ordered Kuropatkin to cancel the withdrawal and instead reinforce Russian forces in the Far East. The fortification of Port Arthur, which had begun in 1900, would be accelerated and the Russian Pacific Squadron would be permanently based there. There would be no deal with Japan about spheres of influence and Witte was kicked upstairs to head the council of ministers; Witte warned the Tsar that, 'an armed clash with Japan would be a great disaster for us'. Witte's counsel was ignored.

Table 1: Build-up of Russian Forces in the Far East, 1895–1903

Year	Troops stationed in Amur Region/Manchuria	Battleships assigned to Pacific Squadron
1895	30,000	1
1898	60,000	2
1901	80,000	3
1903	100,000	7

Table 2: Build-up of Japanese Forces in the Far East, 1895–1903

Year	Active Army (troops)	Battleships in Combined Fleet
1895	90,000	0
1898	140,000	2
1901	150,000	5
1903	180,000	6

Japanese military intelligence officers operating covertly in Manchuria noted the appearance of Russian troops on the Yalu and reinforcements arriving in Port Arthur, which clearly demonstrated that Russia had no intention of honouring its agreements. In June 1903, the Japanese leadership met to consider options for responding to the Russian violations. At first there was little enthusiasm for war, and the decision was made to continue diplomatic discussions. However, a number of more junior military leaders did advocate for war and cited a potential window of opportunity to strike before the Russian garrison in Manchuria had grown too large to defeat in a quick campaign. The Trans-Siberian Railroad was not yet fully completed, but once it was, the Russians would be in a better condition to fight a protracted war of attrition. The Japanese were also aware that additional Russian ground and naval forces were en route to the Far East, so further delay might reduce the chances for achieving a solution by military means. By the end of 1903, Japan had sufficient ground and naval forces to wage a rapid offensive campaign to wrest control of the Liaodong Peninsula from Russia, but the margin for success was narrow. If Japan could win a swift campaign in Manchuria and eliminate the Russian Pacific Squadron, it would establish itself as a major regional power and position itself for realization of its own national interests. After much discussion, the Emperor Meiji gave his approval on 5 February 1904 for Japan to attack Russian forces in Manchuria.

CHRONOLOGY

1898

27 March	Russia acquires a 25-year lease on Port Arthur.

1900

18 January	The Russian War Ministry approves construction plans for the fortification of Port Arthur.
29 June	Russian military forces invade Manchuria in response to Chinese attacks on the China Eastern Railway (CER).
17 September	Russian military forces complete occupation of Manchuria.

1902

8 April	Russia agrees to withdraw its military forces from Manchuria over an 18-month period.

1903

15 May	Tsar orders the strengthening of Russian military forces in the Amur Military District.
23 June	Japan's leadership discusses war with Russia over Manchuria.
18 July	The 4th East Siberian Rifle Brigade is sent to reinforce Port Arthur.
30 October	The 7th East Siberian Rifle Brigade arrives in Port Arthur.

1904

5 February	Emperor Meiji agrees to initiate war with Russia.
6 February	Japan severs diplomatic relations with Russia.
8/9 February	Japan conducts a surprise naval attack on the Russian fleet at Port Arthur.
10 February	The Amur Military District orders all East Siberian Rifle Brigades immediately upgraded to division status.
24 February	First Japanese blockship operation fails.
10 and 22 March	Japanese battleships bombard Port Arthur.
27 March	Second Japanese blockship operation fails.
13 April	Admiral Makarov is lost on the battleship *Petropavlovsk*.
15 April	Alekseyev orders the Pacific Fleet to dismount guns to help defend Port Arthur.
27 April	Alekseyev issues orders for the defence of Port Arthur, which create confusion about command authorities.
2/3 May	Third Japanese blockship operation fails.
5 May	The Japanese Second Army begins landing on the Liaodong Peninsula; Alekseyev leaves for Mukden.
11 May	The Japanese sever Port Arthur's rail line of communications to Liaoyang.
15 May	Togo loses two of his battleships to mines off Port Arthur.
26 May	Japanese victory at the Battle of Nanshan.
28 May	Stackelberg is order to relieve Port Arthur.

6 June	Japanese Third Army becomes operational.
15 June	Stackelberg's effort to relieve Port Arthur is defeated at the Battle of Te-li-ssu.
	Russian cruiser sinks Japanese freighter carrying siege guns to Port Arthur.
23 June	Abortive sortie of Russian fleet from Port Arthur.
26–28 July	The Third Army attacks and forces the Russians to abandon their forward defence on the 'Green Hills'.
30 July	Japanese capture Wolf Hill.
7–9 August	Japanese capture Big Orphan and Little Orphan hills.
10 August	Battle of the Yellow Sea.
16 August	Japanese offer surrender terms.
19–23 August	Nogi launches his first general assault on the Port Arthur defences, capturing 174-metre Hill.
1 September	Third Army begins constructing approach saps.
18–22 September	Nogi launches second general assault on a narrower front, capturing the Water Works and Temple Hill redoubts.
1 October	First 28cm howitzer fired against Port Arthur.
26–30 October	Nogi launches his third general assault, which fails to capture forts II and III.
26–30 November	First phase of Nogi's fourth general assault fails.
5 December	203-metre Hill is finally captured.
5–9 December	Japanese siege artillery demolishes most of the Russian fleet in Port Arthur.
15 December	Kondratenko is killed.
18 December	Fort Chikuan (Fort II) is captured.
28 December	Fort Erhlung (Fort III) is captured.
31 December	Fort Sungshu (Fortification No. 3) surrenders.

1905

1 January	Stoessel seeks terms to surrender.
5 January	Port Arthur surrenders.

OPPOSING COMMANDERS

JAPANESE

The Imperial Japanese Army (IJA – *Dai-Nippon Teikoku Rikugun*) was created as a result of the Meiji Restoration in 1868, which was a concerted effort to end over two centuries of control by the Tokugawa Shogunate and set Japan on the path towards national modernization. Of course, the armies of the Shogunate did not agree to meekly surrender their traditional Samurai privileges and accede to imperial control, but instead fought bitterly to oppose the revolutionary changes during the Boshin War of 1868–69 and again during the Satsuma Rebellion in 1877. Yet even after breaking up the feudal armies of the Shogunate, creating a new national army was no simple task since Japan had heretofore possessed only provincial troops under local *daimyo* (lords). The shift to a system of universal conscription in 1872, followed by the adoption of Western military methods and equipment, was anathema to the traditional Samurai class. Most of the officers that formed the IJA in the Russo-Japanese War were scions of Samurai families who had adapted to the new circumstances. However, clan rivalries and regional sympathies were still a factor in officer selection. While many of these officers had received training on the latest military theories abroad in Europe and at home, much of the new knowledge had not been fully digested. Indeed, the IJA remained a relatively small, amateurish force until the Sino-Japanese War (1894–95) and the Boxer Rebellion (1900); few officers had commanded more than 5,000 troops in combat. Despite relatively easy victories against the Qing Dynasty and two decades of modernization efforts, the IJA in 1904 was still relatively untested and had yet to meet a first-rate opponent in the field.

Vice Admiral Togo Heihachiro, commander-in-chief of the Combined Fleet.

Vice Admiral Togo Heihachiro (1848–1934), commander-in-chief of the Combined Fleet, played a major role in naval operations around Port Arthur. Although well trained in Great Britain, Togo had relatively limited command experience at sea, aside from commanding a cruiser during the Sino-Japanese War, and had never led a large naval force before. Nor did Togo have any experience in operational or campaign planning, even though that was an essential requirement at Port Arthur. Togo had been schooled as a blue-water sailor who longed for a decisive naval surface action in the tradition of Nelson, to whom he constantly compared himself. However, the mission at Port Arthur required a brown-water sailor, with aptitude for such mundane tasks as blockade, escorting convoys and naval gunfire support. Togo proved ineffective in these roles but was the beneficiary of a fawning British press, who saw in him a validation of their own naval traditions. Togo also had a hard, brutal edge in his command persona, which was often glossed over. Despite studying international law during one of his lengthy shore tours, his role in the 1894 Kowshing Incident was akin to a war crime. Furthermore, Togo had no qualms about recommending a surprise naval attack without declaration of war, which contravened contemporary conventions on warfare. In the long run, Togo proved extremely lucky in that the Russian Baltic Fleet presented itself in a disorganized mess at Tsushima, allowing his Combined Fleet to massacre its novice crews. Consequently, Togo is remembered for what he did right at Tsushima, not for what he did wrong at Port Arthur.

General Oku Yasukata (1847–1930) was the commander of the Second Army at the Battle of Nanshan. Oku had risen through the ranks of the late 19th-century IJA, seeing his fair share of combat. By the start of the Russo-Japanese War, Oku was a competent division commander but somewhat out of his depth as an army commander. Like most senior Japanese army officers at this time, Oku had limited appreciation for what modern firepower could accomplish on the battlefield.

General Nogi Maresuke (1849–1912) commanded the Third Army during the siege of Port Arthur. Nogi came from a traditional Samurai family and entered the Imperial Army in 1871, despite having lost sight in one eye due to a childhood accident. He saw combat in the Satsuma Rebellion in 1877, but suffered great disgrace by losing the Emperor's colours in one action, which weighed heavily upon him for the rest of his military career. In 1887–88, he was sent to Germany for 18 months to study its military methods, but upon returning to Japan his career started to unravel for a variety of reasons, including excessive drinking. Nevertheless, during the First Sino-Japanese War, Nogi led an infantry brigade in the capture of Lüshunkou in 1894, and there is no doubt that the rapid success of this operation influenced his plan of action when presented with the same mission in 1904. Afterwards, he was promoted to command of the 2nd Infantry Division, which he led in the conquest of Formosa in 1895. He then served as military governor of Formosa for a year, but allegedly retired from the service in 1897 due to ill health. Nogi spent most of the period 1897–1903 in a semi-retired status. Nevertheless, the IJA was so short of senior commanders that he was recalled to service after the start of the Russo-Japanese War and given command of the Third Army in May 1904. Both of Nogi's sons served in Third Army and both were killed in the Port Arthur campaign. As a commander, Nogi was quite unimaginative and possessed only rudimentary military skills; for example, he could not understand contour lines on a military map. He was a strong believer in frontal attacks and ill-suited to command a complex siege operation. Even many of his contemporaries regarded him as an incompetent commander, who was profligate in expending the lives of his troops and unable to grasp modern warfare.

General Oku Yasukata, commander of the Second Army. (Author's collection)

General Nogi Maresuke, commander of the Third Army at Port Arthur. Despite having been out to pasture prior to the war, Nogi was selected to lead the operation against Port Arthur because of his experience in quickly capturing the port from the Chinese in 1894. (Author's collection)

RUSSIAN

The Imperial Russian Army (*Russkaya imperatorskaya armiya*) was a much larger and heterogenous organization than the IJA. After defeat in the Crimean War, the Russian Army began an extended period of modernization in the 1860s, which continued over the next four decades. In 1875, the Russian Army began modernizing along Prussian lines – creating corps-size formations and establishing a professional officer education system. The *genshtabisty*, or officers who attended the Nikolaev Academy of the General Staff, were intended to be the new elite, although they never comprised more than a fraction of the total officer corps. Most of the officers continued to come from the minor nobility, but it was becoming more common for aspirants from non-Russian ethnic families and non-noble backgrounds to be accepted, at least in the technical branches like the artillery and engineers. The enlisted ranks were also changing as more troops were literate and came from urban rather than rural backgrounds. In terms of combat, the Russian military leaders of 1904 were shaped by their experiences in the Russo-Turkish War of 1877, the conquest of Central Asia in the 1880s and the Boxer Rebellion, all of which emphasized mobility and offensive action.

Vice Admiral Yevgeni I. Alekseyev (1843–1917) was appointed by the Tsar in 1903 as viceroy in the Far East, with broad military-civil authorities. At the start of the Russo-Japanese War, he was headquartered with his administrative staff in Port Arthur and was designated as the theatre commander. Alekseyev was a career naval officer with close personal ties to the Tsar, but otherwise he had no real experience in joint military operations and had difficulty formulating coherent orders and plans. Alekseyev hurriedly departed Port Arthur with his staff in the aftermath of the Japanese naval attack on the Pacific Fleet, then returned for three weeks, until finally leaving for good in early May when a Japanese landing on the Liaodong Peninsula was imminent. While in Port Arthur, Alekseyev issued vague and confusing orders for the defence of the base which left individual command responsibilities in doubt. It would have been simple for Alekseyev to clarify the respective roles of Stoessel and Smirnov, but he did not. Alekseyev was typical of the incompetent cronies that Tsar Nicholas II placed in positions of great authority and his lack of effective command guidance seriously undermined the defence of Port Arthur and the entire Russian war effort in the Far East.

General Aleksei N. Kuropatkin (1848–1925) commanded the Manchuria Army from 7 February 1904. From a noble family near Pskov, Kuropatkin was commissioned as an infantry officer in 1864 and saw action in both the Russo-Turkish War (1877–78) and the Russian conquest of Central Asia. Kuropatkin was a soldier-scholar who was groomed for higher command; he received General Staff training and spent time as a military attaché in France. Kuropatkin moved up rapidly and was made war minister in 1898. Over the next five years, he tried – with limited success – to guide the reform process in the Tsarist Army. Kuropatkin was also responsible for approving plans for the fortification

General-leytenant Anatoli M. Stoessel assumed command at Port Arthur in March 1904, and would not relinquish command despite orders from the Tsar and Kuropatkin. In the pantheon of military history, Stoessel set a standard for incompetence which has rarely been challenged.

of Port Arthur and the Liaodong Peninsula, although he did not push for any urgency in the construction programme. Unlike Russian naval leaders, Kuropatkin regarded Port Arthur as a liability that would be difficult to sustain in wartime. He also recognized Japan's increased military capabilities after attending their summer manoeuvres in 1903, but his warnings were disregarded in St Petersburg. Unable to halt the slide to war, Kuropatkin resigned his post as minister of war. At the outbreak of war in the Far East, Kuropatkin was sent to take command of all Russian ground forces in Manchuria. Appreciating Russia's logistical difficulties in sustaining large-scale military operations in the Far East, Kuropatkin preferred to wage a cautious defensive campaign until massively reinforced. While personally brave, Kuropatkin often proved unwilling to make difficult decisions or take excessive risks, preferring to play it safe – even if it meant leaving the garrison in Port Arthur to its own devices. However, neither the Tsar nor Alekseyev would allow Kuropatkin to remain on the defensive while Port Arthur was invested, which placed him in a serious dilemma.

General-leytenant Anatoli M. Stoessel (1848–1915) was commander of the III Siberian Army Corps at Port Arthur from August 1903. Like many career officers in the Tsarist Army, Stoessel was a nobleman of ethnic German lineage. While Stoessel had a fairly distinguished record as an infantry officer over the course of over 30 years, he had no real experience with independent command nor led any formation larger than a regiment. Nevertheless, like many Tsarist officers, he knew how to work political and court connections to get choice assignments. Lacking real military skill or judgement, Stoessel was prone to panic; during the Boxer Rebellion, he once ordered a precipitate retreat when his regiment encountered Chinese firecrackers. Consequently, Stoessel was a poor choice to command Russia's key fortified naval base in the Far East, which Kuropatkin tried to correct before the siege proper began. However, Stoessel obstinately refused to step aside in favour of Smirnov and defied his chain of command. Arrogant, incompetent and cowardly, Stoessel was the epitome of command failure.

General-mayor Aleksandr V. Fok, commander of the 4th East Siberian Rifle Division. Fok consistently managed to snatch defeat from successful Russian defensive actions by refusing reserves and ordering unauthorized retreats at critical moments.

General-leytenant Konstantin Smirnov (1854–1930) was appointed fortress commander at Port Arthur by Alekseyev on 15 February 1904, but he did not arrive until 17 March. Alekseyev issued confusing orders in April that Smirnov would command the fortress (which was effectively Port Arthur and approaches), while Stoessel would continue to command his rifle corps in the Liaodong Peninsula. Smirnov was a career artillery officer, trained at the elite Nikolaev Academy, experienced in defensive tactics and energetic. However, Stoessel chose to interpret Alekseyev's order in such a way that Smirnov would be subordinate to him. Unfortunately, Smirnov lacked the moral courage to ignore Stoessel and simply take command at Port Arthur, as ordered by both the Tsar and Kuropatkin. Instead, Smirnov did what he could to assist the defence but otherwise allowed himself to be shoved aside by a less capable officer – which is a form of dereliction of duty.

General-mayor Aleksandr V. Fok (1843–1926) was the commander of the 4th East Siberian Rifle Division

stationed at Port Arthur. Fok was commissioned as an infantry officer in 1864 and had been honoured for valour in the Russo-Turkish War and recognized for his leadership of the 4th East Siberian Rifle Brigade during the Boxer Rebellion. On paper, Fok appeared to be competent and he cultivated a close relationship with Stoessel, who held him in high regard. Nevertheless, Fok proved to be thoroughly incompetent and gutless in his role as a rifle division commander, contributing in great measure to the Russian defeat.

General-leytenant Roman I. Kondratenko (1857–1904) was commander of the 7th East Siberian Rifle Division, stationed in Port Arthur from 1903. Unlike most of the other senior Russian commanders, Kondratenko was an ethnic Ukrainian and not from the minor nobility. Indeed, Kondratenko was a self-made man who was commissioned in the engineers in 1879 and had received General Staff training. Assigned to command an infantry brigade in the Far East in November 1903, Kondratenko demonstrated a good grasp of modern tactics and was innovative in looking for equipment and tactics to boost the power of the defence. Throughout the siege, Kondratenko set a fine example as a front-line combat leader and avoided the political bickering among Stoessel, Smirnov and other petty officers in the garrison. However, Kondratenko lacked the social cachet to stand up to the wrong-headed decisions of officers like Fok, which hamstrung his ability to conduct an effective defence.

Polkovnik Nikolai A. Tretyakov (1854–1917) had been the commander of the 5th East Siberian Rifle Regiment from 1901. Tretyakov was commissioned as an engineer officer in 1875. His organization of the blocking position at Nanshan Hill set new standards for defensive warfare that would reappear on the Western Front in 1914–18. Despite his low rank, Tretyakov also played a major role in the defence of Port Arthur, being responsible for Sector II (the western front).

General-mayor Vladimir N. Gorbatovsky (1851–1924) commanded the 1st Brigade of the 7th East Siberian Rifle Division and Sector I of Port Arthur's inner defence. Gorbatovsky was a veteran infantry officer who led from the front and helped to stabilize the situation at key moments in the siege.

OPPOSING FORCES

JAPANESE

Both the IJA and IJN had expanded rapidly since the end of the Sino-Japanese War. By early 1904, Japan's active army was 180,000 strong, with another 200,000 trained reserves available, which translated into 13 infantry divisions (one of which was the Imperial Guards) and about a dozen Kobi (reserve) brigades. Lieutenant-General Kodama intended to employ two field armies (the First and Second) in the opening phase of the war. After full mobilization, the Third and Fourth armies would be established and additional reserve infantry brigades would be sent to reinforce the field armies, but the Japanese could not afford to sustain excessive casualties if they were to retain the strategic initiative in Manchuria. Likewise, Togo's Combined Fleet had a small margin of superiority over the Russian Pacific Squadron, but he would have to detach warships to monitor the independent Russian cruiser squadron in Vladivostok as well as to protect the sea lines of communication back to Japan.

Although General Oku Yasukata's Second Army was the formation tasked with landing on the Liaodong Peninsula, its primary purpose was to push on to Liaoyang, not seize Port Arthur. Instead, after dealing with the Nanshan Hill position, the Second Army detached the 1st Infantry Division to blockade the peninsula until Nogi's Third Army arrived in August. Ultimately, the IJA committed four infantry divisions (1st, 7th, 9th and 11th) and two reserve Kobi infantry brigades to the siege of Port Arthur, which afforded the Third Army only a 2:1 numerical advantage over the Russian defenders. Each Japanese infantry division comprised four infantry regiments (each with a nominal total of 3,145 men, subdivided into three battalions, each of four companies), an artillery regiment (of two battalions, each with 18 75mm field guns), a cavalry regiment (435 troops) and an engineer battalion

Japanese infantry deployed on line in a trench, probably during training, summer 1904. The troops are wearing the new khaki uniform and their kit looks very new and clean. Note the junior officers squatting behind the trenches, with drawn swords. (Nik Cornish/Stavka)

The Third Army was provided with 40 Hotchkiss machine guns at the start of the campaign but found them difficult to employ in the attack. Eventually, the Japanese figured out how to move machine guns forward to help secure positions that had been captured by their infantry, in order to defeat Russian counter-attacks. (Author's collection)

(700 troops); with a nominal overall strength of about 15,000 troops. The Kobi reserve brigades had six infantry battalions, but negligible support troops. Altogether, Nogi's Third Army had a paper strength of about 80,000 troops, of which 75 per cent were infantrymen.

The IJA's main strength was its infantry, which were fairly well trained by contemporary standards. Japanese infantry units were usually larger than the opposing Russian infantry units, with about 1,000 troops in a battalion and 250 in a company. Most of the active-duty Japanese infantrymen shifted to the new khaki field uniform just prior to the beginning of the siege, but reserve and support troops arrived still wearing the M1886 blue uniform. Since 1897, the Japanese infantry had been re-equipping with the 6.5mm Type 30 Arisaka rifle, which was a big improvement over the 11mm Type 18 Murata rifle used in the Sino-Japanese War. Nevertheless, Japan was struggling to adapt foreign weapons designs for indigenous production and the Type 30 Arisaka rifle was distinctly inferior to the Russian Mosin-Nagant rifle in a number of important respects. In order to supplement its infantry firepower, the IJA leadership began considering the French-made 8mm Hotchkiss M1897 machine gun, but decided that they wanted their support weapon to use the same 6.5mm round as the Arisaka rifle. By 1901, Hotchkiss was able to provide the IJA with five 6.5mm prototypes and licensed production began at the Tokyo Arsenal. However, only a small number of Hotchkiss (Hoshiki) machine guns were available at the start of the Russo-Japanese War. In late August 1904, the Third Army received 40 Hotchkiss machine guns (some mounted on tripods, others on wheeled carriages with bulletproof shields). The IJA divisions had not trained with machine guns prior to the campaign and commanders were uncertain how to employ them in the attack. Furthermore, the Hotchkiss used 30-round metallic ammunition strips, which resulted in a significantly lower volume of fire than the Russian belt-fed Maxim machine guns.

Japanese soldiers went to war in 1904 infused with a potent mix of nationalism and Shinto religion, intended to create *Yamato-damashii*

('Japanese spirit'). Japanese tactical leaders were extremely aggressive and opted for rapid manoeuvre and frontal assaults, even when conditions were unfavourable. Yet in terms of infantry tactics, the Japanese had not yet learned what modern firepower could do and their assault formations tended to 'bunch up' and advance in large groups. Compared to the Russians, the Japanese infantry had relatively anaemic organic firepower and were thus inclined to seek combat resolution at close quarters – which guaranteed heavy losses.

The IJA had not employed field artillery much during the Sino-Japanese War, and thus its experience with this branch was still based primarily on theory provided by European advisors. In order to capture a fortified position such as Port Arthur, it was clear that the Third Army would require effective artillery support, but pre-war efforts to improve this branch fell short of actual requirements. Japanese field artillery batteries had just been re-equipped with the 75mm field gun Type 31 (M1898), which was something of an interim design, particularly in terms of its primitive recoil system. While the Type 31 gun could fire high explosive (HE) rounds filled with Shimosa (similar to the French Melinite explosive), only 12 per cent of ammunition was HE, the rest was shrapnel. Shimosa was something of a Japanese secret weapon, which was capable of producing a powerful blast effect, but it was also very unstable and premature explosions were not uncommon. Usually, each Japanese infantry regiment in the assault was supported by at least one field artillery battery with six 75mm guns, and often additional batteries were provided by an army-level artillery brigade. The IJA staff officers also seriously underestimated how much artillery ammunition it would require for an extended campaign, and domestic production was only about 15,000 rounds of 75mm per month. Additional rounds were purchased in Europe, but they did not arrive until December 1904. The shortage of artillery ammunition would have a disruptive impact upon the Japanese operational tempo at Port Arthur and the larger campaign in Manchuria, as well.

Rather surprisingly, the IJA leadership had not put any real thought into forming a siege train prior to hostilities (another example of deficient planning). Instead, the Third Army was forced to improvise a heavy artillery group once the siege was already underway. The only artillery suitable for siege work immediately available were domestically built 9cm and 15cm mortars, which were rather primitive. About 74 modern heavy artillery pieces were purchased from Krupp after the war started, including some 12cm and 15cm howitzers and some 12cm field guns, although most did not arrive until the final months of the siege. The IJN contributed a number of 4.7in./40 QF (12cm) guns on ground mounts to the Third Army, which were used to shell Port Arthur from a distance. However, the Japanese trump card at Port Arthur proved to be the 28cm

The Japanese division-level artillery was based upon the Type 31 75mm field gun, introduced in 1898. The gun could fire high explosive (HE) or shrapnel rounds but did not have a high rate of fire since it lacked a recoil system. (Author's collection)

Nogi owed his victory at Port Arthur to the three batteries of 28cm siege howitzers that demolished the Russian fortified positions one after another. However, the 28cm siege howitzer was designed as a coastal defence weapon and required extensive engineering effort to emplace, and the Japanese had to conceal these positions to protect them from Russian counter-battery fire. (Author's collection)

howitzer L/10, which had been developed from an Italian design (which itself was a copy of a British design) as a coast defence weapon. Between October and December 1904, three six-gun batteries with 28cm howitzers were sent to the Third Army. The 28cm howitzer weighed 40 tons in action and required extensive engineering support to emplace, but its 217kg shells could crush Russian fortified positions and even sink battleships. However, poor quality control in the manufacturing of ammunition for the 28cm guns led to 25 per cent of these rounds failing to explode in combat.

The Japanese Third Army had three division-level engineer battalions at Port Arthur, as well as some bridging and sapper troops. At the start of the war, Japanese engineers were expected to bridge water obstacles and repair roads, but they had no training in clearing mines or barbed wire – all that would have to be learned on the battlefield. Indeed, the IJA really had no prior experience with common siege-warfare techniques, such as digging saps. During the later stages of the siege of Port Arthur, Japanese sappers were also required to dig tunnels through solid rock in order to emplace explosive charges underneath Russian forts. The other Japanese support branches in the Third Army – signal telegraph, medical, transport and quartermasters – totalled only about 5 per cent of the available personnel and consisted mostly of reservists and recent conscripts. The amount of transport, food and ammunition provided to the Third Army was barely adequate for a protracted siege, but division and army commanders looked with disdain upon support troops and paid little heed to logistic issues. Japanese troops were allowed to consume contaminated water and rice, which resulted in nearly 15 per cent of Nogi's troops being laid low by illnesses such as typhoid and dysentery.

Togo's Combined Fleet played a major role in the siege of Port Arthur, including torpedo attacks, naval bombardment, mining operations and blockship operations, while simultaneously maintaining a blockade of the port. For the most part, Togo relied on his light units to conduct close-in operations in order to reduce the risk to his battleships from enemy mines and coastal artillery. The most useful vessels for naval gunfire support tended to be gunboats (armed with 12cm main guns and 4.7cm QF guns) and destroyers (armed with 76mm and 57mm QF guns), both types of which had draughts of 2–4m. However, the IJN had virtually no minesweeping capabilities, which proved to be a serious problem in the shallow, mine-infested waters around Port Arthur.

RUSSIAN

Prior to the war, most Russian troops stationed in the Far East were subordinate to the Amur Military District, with its headquarters in Khabarovsk. The area around Port Arthur and the southern Liaodong

Peninsula was designated as the Kwantung Fortified Area (*Kvantunskiy ukreplonnyy rayon*). Although there were about 140,000 Russian troops in or near Manchuria, they were dispersed over an area that was roughly the size of the UK. The main clusters were 45,000 troops near Vladivostok, 28,000 near Harbin and 24,000 troops near Port Arthur. However, over 35,000 troops were spread out protecting the length of the CER from Chinese armed bandits (known as Honghuzi) and the largest tactical units in theatre were the eight East Siberian Rifle brigades, each with about 3,000 troops. At the start of the war in February 1904, all the disparate Russian ground forces in the region were put under Kuropatkin's newly formed Manchuria Army, while Vice Admiral Alekseyev became overall theatre commander. Within days of the Japanese naval attack on Port Arthur, the Amur Military District ordered all East Siberian Rifle brigades upgraded to division status, by the infusion of reserves and other personnel (such as frontier guards, militiamen and railway guards). Just before the Japanese declaration of war, the Russian War Ministry began mobilizing some reserve battalions in the western military districts, in order to reinforce the East Siberian units and these troops were soon en route to the Far East.

During the period 1898–1903, the Russian garrison in Port Arthur consisted of a single infantry regiment (with three battalions) and one battalion of fortress artillery. However, as the likelihood of war increased, the garrison was steadily reinforced, beginning with the arrival in July 1903 of Fok's 4th East Siberian Rifle Brigade, which had seen recent combat during the Boxer Rebellion. In October, the 7th East Siberian Rifle Brigade was sent to Port Arthur, along with more artillery batteries. The East Siberian rifle regiments were expanded from two to three rifle battalions by incorporating personnel from their reserve battalions and through the transfer of individual rifle companies from western Russia. After the Japanese declaration of war, both rifle brigades were rapidly expanded into divisions. Altogether, the 4th and 7th East Siberian Rifle divisions and Tretyakov's independent 5th East Siberian Rifle Regiment comprised 28 rifle battalions and seven field artillery batteries. Eventually, the 41,000-man garrison coalesced into the III Siberian Corps under General-leytenant Anatoli M. Stoessel. Although the Russian mobilization in the Far East was rapid, it left the newly formed divisions in a somewhat unsettled state. The shortage of junior officers was particularly acute. Nevertheless, Russian infantry was very stubborn in the defence and willing to endure heavier losses than most armies.

After full mobilization, each Siberian Rifle Regiment in the garrison had about 3,900 troops organized in three rifle battalions (plus a reserve or depot battalion), each of four rifle companies. A Russian infantry battalion in Manchuria had a nominal wartime strength of about 700 troops and each company 180–240 troops. The best soldiers from each company were combined into a regimental-level scout detachment (*okhotniki*)

A Russian infantry company deployed on line in Manchuria. Thanks to the Mosin-Nagant M1891 rifle, Russian infantrymen had better long-range firepower than Japanese infantry units, although pre-war marksmanship training was inadequate. (Author's collection)

Russian artillerymen with the 76.2mm field gun M1900, which was the first Russian field gun with a recoil system. In combat, the 76mm M1900 field gun could fire 8–10 rounds of HE or shrapnel per minute. (Author's collection)

with roughly 80–100 troops. The Russian infantry was equipped with the modern 7.62mm Mosin-Nagant M1891 rifle (a.k.a. the 'Three Line Rifle, Model 1891'), which was a solid and reliable weapon. The Tsar was particularly impressed with the Mosin-Nagant and thought that it would provide Russian infantry with an advantage in long-range firepower on the battlefield. While the Mosin-Nagant offered a potential advantage in firepower, the fact that the Russian Army allotted only 20 rounds per soldier for annual weapon qualification and did not place any great emphasis upon rifle marksmanship tended to undermine this technical edge. Furthermore, the Russian Army retained a lingering 'cult of the bayonet' which placed greater emphasis on close-quarter combat rather than long-range rifle fire.

The new Maxim machine gun also offered a great technical advance in battlefield firepower, but its adoption by the Russian Army was problematic. In 1888, the Russian War Ministry purchased its first Maxim machine guns (initially chambered for the 10.67mm Berdan cartridge, but converted to 7.62mm in 1892) but delayed adopting the weapon for service use until 1901. During the Boxer Rebellion, the Russian expeditionary force gained some experience with the Maxim gun in combat and was impressed by its ability to slaughter massed Chinese militia attacks. As a result, over 200 Maxim machine guns were purchased from Vickers (at a price of 2,288 rubles each), but they were assigned to the Main Artillery Directorate, which intended to use them for the defence of fortresses, not support infantry in field battles. Indeed, the artillerymen decided to mount the Maxim machine gun on a wheeled carriage, which had a total weight of 244kg. Nevertheless, by 1904 the Russian Army had formed five machine-gun companies (each with eight Maxim machine guns) to attach to rifle divisions – but only one of these companies was in the Far East, attached to the 3rd East Siberian Rifle Brigade in Port Arthur. Since it was designated as a fortress, the garrison in Port Arthur was eventually assigned 62 machine guns – roughly 20 per cent of the entire inventory then in service. The belt-fed Maxim machine gun, which could fire up to 300 rounds per minute, would prove to be the main Russian trump card in the siege of Port Arthur, and its defensive firepower was impressive.

On paper, the Russian garrison in Port Arthur had 136 field guns at the start of the war, as well as 108 coastal defence guns. In reality, Stoessel's III East Siberian Rifle Corps had just seven field artillery batteries (each equipped with eight 87mm M1877 field guns), two mountain artillery batteries (each with eight Baranovsky 63mm guns), plus an assortment of minor detachments equipped with 152mm field mortars and captured Chinese artillery pieces. The Russian field artillery branch was in a state of flux in early 1904, with the obsolescent Krupp-designed 87mm M1877 field gun in the process of being replaced by the modern 76.2mm M1900 and M1902 guns (designed by Putilov). While the Putilov field gun offered 30 per cent better range and five times the rate of fire of the 87mm guns it was replacing, very few were in the Far East in February 1904 and only a few M1900 guns reached Port Arthur. The East Siberian artillerymen also had the obsolescent 42-line M1877 siege gun, a 106mm weapon that was ill suited for field battles. Most of the Russian field artillery was only capable of direct fire missions and relied on shrapnel and HE shells filled with picric acid; neither of these shells were particularly effective against entrenched troops. Incredibly, the Russian Main Artillery Directorate did not conduct pre-war tests to verify the lethality of their exploding munitions, in order to save money. Likewise, Kuropatkin had wanted to test the new ammunition and reorganize the artillery into eight-gun batteries, but the Tsar took 3 million rubles from the artillery modernization budget, ostensibly to spend on supplemental tea rations for the troops (there was quite a lot of graft in the Romanov war machine, often disguised as such expenditures).

Port Arthur's coastal defence was the responsibility of three fortress artillery battalions, but these formations were short of trained personnel and not all batteries could be effectively manned. The most impressive battery was No. 15 on the 'Electric Cliff', where five 10in./45 M1891 cannons mounted in concrete barbettes guarded the southern approaches to the port. Three batteries (2nd, 9th and 19th) with a total of 15 modern French-designed (Canet) 6in. M1892 guns were also extant. However, the fire arcs of the coastal batteries were often restricted by the mountainous terrain, and there was 'dead space' that could only be covered by the heavy mortars – which proved unable to hit moving ships. Even worse, through an idiotic mistake, no armour-piercing ammunition had been issued to the coastal batteries – only cast-iron training shells – which rendered much of the coastal artillery defence impotent. At night, the coastal artillery was dependent upon searchlights to illuminate targets, but only three 90cm searchlights were

A Russian coastal artillery battery protecting the entrance to Port Arthur. In a major mistake, the batteries were not issued with armour-piercing (AP) ammunition prior to the outbreak of war. Eventually, the Pacific Squadron was ordered to provide the batteries with some AP ammunition. (Author's collection)

The two most useful warships in the Russian Pacific Squadron were the minelayers *Amur* and *Yenisei*, which were each capable of laying up to 300 contact mines. In the shallow waters around Port Arthur, minefields proved to be effective in protecting the entrance to the harbour and inflicting losses on the Japanese blockading fleet. (Author's collection)

available to the garrison in February 1904. The remainder of Port Arthur's coastal artillery consisted of older, less effective weapons, including 22 9in. (229mm) and ten 11in. (280mm) coastal mortars M1877, 12 6in. (152mm) M1877 fortress guns, four 4.2in. (106mm) M1877 field guns and 28 57mm QF guns. Only seven of 22 coastal defence batteries were completed at the start of the war, with the rest in various stages of construction – which meant that little gunnery training was conducted prior to the war.

The Russian engineers under Polkovnik Apollon A. Grigorenko played a key role in developing the system of fortifications around Port Arthur. Grigorenko had a 420-man fortress sapper company, but few of its personnel were trained. Nevertheless, with the help of infantry units, Grigorenko's sappers were able to fortify the position at Nanshan with entrenchments and barbed wire. What the Russian sappers lacked in experience they made up for with creativity and imagination. During the siege of Port Arthur, the Russian sappers would develop and use several types of electrically detonated command mines, wooden pressure mines and other improvised explosive devices. The Russian sappers also used naval mines to defend critical land positions. In addition, Russian sappers became adept at counter-mining to prevent Japanese sappers from tunnelling underneath forward positions.

The support services in Port Arthur were of varied quality and the departure of Alekseyev's administrative staff undermined efforts to organize for a protracted siege. Although there was one signal-telegraph company stationed in the fortress, minimal effort was made to establish wire communications with positions in the outer defensive perimeter prior to the beginning of the siege. Those telephone lines that were in place were placed above ground and easily severed by enemy artillery fire. As the siege progressed, the Russians did establish buried field telephone links with key forward positions, but the ability to coordinate with artillery batteries was further hindered by the limited number of telephones. In terms of medical services, the Russian Red Cross (*Rossiyskogo Obshchestva Krasnogo Kresta*, or ROKK) was able to send several well-funded field hospital units to Port Arthur before the base was isolated (which had the capability to use X-ray devices – a first in military medicine) and three freighters (*Angara*, *Kazan* and *Mongolia*) were transferred to the ROKK and converted into hospital ships. Normally, disease is a factor in siege warfare, and there would be problems with typhus among the garrison, but the Russian medical services were able to limit the effects of illness and malnutrition on the front-line troops until nearly the end of the siege. In terms of logistical services, the Russian quartermasters had laid in enough food stocks and medical supplies to withstand a six-month siege. Furthermore, fishing in local waters provided a safety net against absolute starvation – a fact that Togo did not understand. The Japanese naval blockade around Port Arthur was never air-tight and blockade runners were able to bring in some additional supplies, as well. Ammunition stockpiles were adequate, with 31.9 million rounds of 7.62mm small-arms cartridges on hand, as well as a decent stock of most types of artillery ammunition.

In February 1904, Vice Admiral Oskar V. Stark's Pacific Squadron stationed in Port Arthur had seven battleships, five cruisers, 25 destroyers, eight gunboats and several auxiliary vessels, including the minelayers *Amur* and *Yenisei*. The total crews for all these vessels amounted to roughly 10,000 sailors, or more than twice the civilian population of Port Arthur. Contrary to pre-war expectations, it was not the battleships that contributed the most to the defence of Port Arthur, but the minelayers and shallow-draft gunboats. The Japanese had very limited ability to find and neutralize Russian moored contact mines and these weapons came very close to being a game-changer at Port Arthur. The two Amur-class minelayers were the first purpose-built ocean-going minelayers in the world and were each capable of laying up to 400 contact mines. Gunboats could also manoeuvre close to shore in the shallow waters around Port Arthur to provide fire support. In contrast, once it became apparent that the capital ships were trapped and nearly useless in Port Arthur, a steady process of removing weapons and crews from the immobilized vessels to support the ground defence began. In particular, the 37mm and 47mm Hotchkiss QF guns were well-suited for ground mounting, and virtually all of the Maxim machine guns in the fleet were transferred ashore.

ORDERS OF BATTLE

JAPANESE

THIRD ARMY (GENERAL NOGI MARESUKE)

Chief of Staff (Major-General Ijichi Kosuke)
Chief of Artillery (Major-General Toyoshima Yozo)
Chief of Intelligence (Lieutenant-Colonel Kumaji Yamaoka)
Chief of Logistics (Lieutenant-Colonel Inoue Ikutaro)
1st Infantry Division (Lieutenant-General Tsumumoto Matsumura)[1]
1st Infantry Brigade (Major-General Yamamoto Nobuyuki)[2]
    1st Infantry Regiment (Lieutenant-Colonel Terada Sakurui)[3]
    15th Infantry Regiment (Lieutenant-Colonel Okubo Naomichi)
2nd Infantry Brigade (Major-General Nakamura Satoru)[4]
    2nd Infantry Regiment (Lieutenant-Colonel Watanabe Kijuro)
    3rd Infantry Regiment (Lieutenant-Colonel Ushijima Honban)

1st Field Artillery Regiment (Colonel Masataka Hyodo)
1st Cavalry Regiment (Lieutenant-Colonel Nawa Naganori)
1st Engineer Battalion (Colonel Oki Fusanosuke)
9th Infantry Division (Lieutenant-General Oshima Hisanao)
6th Infantry Brigade (Major-General Ichinohe Hyoe)
    7th Infantry Regiment (Colonel Ouchi Mamoru Shizuka)[5]
    35th Infantry Regiment (Lieutenant-Colonel Orishita Katsuzo)
18th Infantry Brigade (Major-General Hirasara Ryozo)
    19th Infantry Regiment (Lieutenant-Colonel Hattori Naohiko)[6]
    36th Infantry Regiment (Colonel Mihara Shigeo)[7]
9th Field Artillery Regiment (Lieutenant-Colonel Ujita Toranosuke)
9th Cavalry Regiment (Lieutenant-Colonel Hirasa)
9th Engineer Battalion (Lieutenant-Colonel Ashizawa Masakatsu)

1 Died of illness, 5 February 1905.
2 Died of wounds, 24 September 1904.
3 Died on 203-metre Hill, 28 November 1904.
4 Wounded, 26 November 1904.

5 Killed in action, 21 August 1904.
6 Killed in action, 28 November 1904.
7 Killed in action, 27 August 1904.

11th Infantry Division (Lieutenant-General Tsuchiya Mitsuharu)[8]
10th Infantry Brigade (Major-General Yamanaka Nobuyoshi)
    22nd Infantry Regiment (Colonel Aoki Sukejiro)
    44th Infantry Regiment (Colonel Ishihara Roh)
22nd Infantry Brigade (Major-General Kamio Mitsuomi)
    12th Infantry Regiment (Colonel Niiyama Yoshitomo)
    43rd Infantry Regiment (Colonel Nishiyama Yasuyuki)[9]
11th Field Artillery Regiment (Colonel Adachi Aizo)
11th Cavalry Regiment (Lieutenant-Colonel Kawamura Shuichi)
11th Engineer Battalion (Lieutenant-Colonel Ishikawa Kiyotaro)
1st Kobi (Reserve) Infantry Brigade (Major-General Tomoyasu Harunobu)[10]
1st Reserve Infantry Regiment (Lieutenant-Colonel Yogo Masanobu)
15th Reserve Infantry Regiment (Lieutenant-Colonel Katsuki Saburo)
16th Reserve Infantry Regiment (Lieutenant-Colonel Niina Kota)
4th Kobi (Reserve) Infantry Brigade (Major-General Takeuchi Seisaku)
8th Reserve Infantry Regiment (Colonel Mikami Shintaro)
9th Reserve Infantry Regiment (Lieutenant-Colonel Takagi Yoshitaka)
38th Reserve Infantry Regiment (Colonel Takimoto Miki)

2nd Field Artillery Brigade (Major-General Osako Naomichi)
    16th Field Artillery Regiment (Lieutenant-Colonel Narita Masamine)

8 Badly wounded, 26 November 1904.
9 Wounded in action, 26 November 1904.
10 Relieved of command, sometime during November 1904.

17th Field Artillery Regiment (Lieutenant-Colonel Yokota Sotaro)
18th Field Artillery Regiment (Lieutenant-Colonel Honjo Zenno)
1st Field Heavy Artillery Regiment (Lieutenant-Colonel Noboru Eto)
1st Foot Artillery Regiment (Colonel Mikageike Tomokuni)
2nd Foot Artillery Regiment (Lieutenant-Colonel Tadayoshi Kohei)
3rd Foot Artillery Regiment (Colonel Kato Yasuhisa)
1st Independent Artillery Battalion
Naval Brigade (Commander Kuroi Tejiro)
    1st Battery (six 4.7in. QF guns [12cm])
    2nd Battery (16 12-pounders [7.6cm])
    3rd Battery (four 12-pounders [7.6cm])
Reinforcements
1 October 1904
One battery (six) 28cm siege guns
15 October 1904
Two batteries (12) 28cm siege guns
16 November 1904
7th Infantry Division (Lieutenant-General Osako Naotoshi)
    13th Infantry Brigade (Major-General Yoshida Seiichi)
        25th Infantry Regiment (Colonel Watanabe Mizuya)
        26th Infantry Regiment (Lieutenant-Colonel Arata Yoshida)
    14th Infantry Brigade (Major-General Saito Taro)
        27th Infantry Regiment (Lieutenant-Colonel Okuda Masatada)
        28th Infantry Regiment (Colonel Murakami Masamichi)
    7th Field Artillery Regiment (Lieutenant-Colonel Tsurumi Kazuma)
    7th Cavalry Regiment (Lieutenant-Colonel Shiraishi Chiyotaro)
    7th Engineer Battalion (Major Sato Masatake)

RUSSIAN

III SIBERIAN ARMY CORPS (GENERAL-LEYTENANT ANATOLI M. STOESSEL)

Chief of Staff: General-mayor Viktor A. Reis
4th East Siberian Rifle Division (General-mayor Aleksandr V. Fok)
1st Brigade (General-mayor Vitaly E. Andro-de-Buy Ginglatt)[11]
    13th East Siberian Rifle Regiment (three battalions) (Polkovnik Ivan I. Machabeli)[12]
    14th East Siberian Rifle Regiment (three battalions) (Polkovnik Vladimir M. Savitsky)
2nd Brigade (General-mayor Mitrofan A. Nadein)
    15th East Siberian Rifle Regiment (three battalions) (Polkovnik Nikolai P. Gryaznov)
    16th East Siberian Rifle Regiment (three battalions) (Polkovnik Mikhail A. Bem)
4th East Siberian Rifle Artillery Brigade (four batteries with eight 76.2mm guns each) (General-mayor Vladimir A. Irmanov)[13]
7th East Siberian Rifle Division (General-mayor Roman I. Kondratenko)[14]
1st Brigade (General-mayor Vladimir N. Gorbatovsky)
    25th Siberian Rifle Regiment (Podpolkovnik Iosif G. Nekrashevich-Poklad)
    26th Siberian Rifle Regiment (Polkovnik Vladimir G. Semenov)
2nd Brigade (General-mayor Vikenty V. Tserpitsky)[15]
    27th Siberian Rifle Regiment (Polkovnik Kazimir E. Nevyadomsky)
    28th Siberian Rifle Regiment (Polkovnik Moses E. Murman)
    5th East Siberian Rifle Regiment (Polkovnik Nikolai A. Tretyakov)
        One attached battery with eight field guns
7th East Siberian Rifle Artillery Brigade (two batteries with eight 76.2mm guns each) (Polkovnik Samadbek Mehmandarov)

11 Ginglatt, of French-Polish ethnicity, was commander of the brigade until at least mid-June 1904. After that, Ginglatt was transferred to Kuropatkin's staff and Savitsky served as his de facto replacement.
12 Killed in action, 8 August 1904. Replaced by Polkovnik Sergei M. Pospelov.
13 Irmanov became commander of Sector II in the Port Arthur defence.
14 Killed in action, 15 December 1904.
15 Killed in action, 22 November 1904.

KWANTUNG FORTIFIED AREA (GENERAL-LEYTENANT KONSTANTIN SMIRNOV)

Chief of Staff: Polkovnik Alexander M. Khvostov
Artillery Commander: General-mayor Vasily F. Bely
Chief Engineer: Polkovnik Apollon A. Grigorenko
Quartermaster: Kapitan Mikhail I. Dostovalov
Kwantung Fortress Artillery
1st Battalion Fortress Artillery (Podpolkovnik Alexander Vepritsky)
2nd Battalion Fortress Artillery (Polkovnik Grigory L. Stolnikov)
3rd Battalion Fortress Artillery (Polkovnik Nikolai A. Brzhozovsky)

3rd East Siberian Sapper Battalion (four companies)
    Kwantung sapper company (Podpolkovnik Petr E. Zherebtsov, 279 men)
3rd, 4th and 7th East Siberian Reserve Battalions (depot units)
21st and 36th Frontier Guard companies
1st Verkhneudinsky Cossack Regiment (4th Company only)

FIRST PACIFIC SQUADRON (REAR ADMIRAL WILGELM VITGEFT)[16]

Battleships (six): *Sevastopol*, *Peresvet*, *Pobeda*, *Poltava*, *Tsesarevich*, and *Retvizan*
Armoured cruiser (one): *Bayan*
Protected cruisers (five): *Pallada*, *Diana*, *Askold*, *Novik*, and *Boyarin*
Destroyers (25): four Bezstrashni-class, one Boevoi-class, two Boiki-class, five Vnimatelni-class, one Leytant Burakov-class, 12 Puilki-class
Torpedo-gunboats (two): two Kazarski-class
Gunboats (six): two Grozyashchi-class, two Kreiser-class, one Sivuch-class (*Bobr*), *Gilyak*
Minelayer (one): *Amur*

16 Vitgeft was killed on 10 August 1904.

OPPOSING PLANS

JAPANESE

The strategic-level military planning process established in Japan between 1893 and 1904 was amorphous and would continue to pose systemic problems until its final failure in 1945. Foremost was the difficulty in coordinating army and navy strategic plans. Although the Imperial General Headquarters (Daihonei) had been established in 1893 and included senior members of both the army and naval general staffs, it only existed in wartime, which meant that each service conducted pre-war planning on its own. Joint doctrine is best established in peacetime and practised in wargames, but in Meiji Japan each service followed its own path and developed strategies which suited their own organizational objectives: the army raised new divisions and the navy bought new battleships. How these divisions and battleships should be best used to achieve Japan's strategic objectives was not really discussed in detail. The second problem was that the Emperor Meiji was nominally in charge of the military, but he really only approved or disapproved plans presented by the Military Council, which included members from the Daihonei, as well as the army and navy ministers and foreign minister. Under this system, the emperor received rather narrow options based mostly on military capabilities applied to specific scenarios, rather than encompassing a full strategic picture. As a result, Japanese strategy tended to be short term in nature and viewed through service-specific prisms.

In October 1903, Lieutenant-General Kodama Gentaro, deputy chief of the IJA's general staff, began planning for war with Russia, with the approval of his boss, Field Marshal Oyama Iwao. Thanks to an excellent espionage network established in Manchuria, the IJA's General Staff had a fairly good picture of Russian military forces in the Far East. Kodama knew that Japan had a 3:2 numerical advantage in ground troops, but this edge would quickly dissipate as soon as large-scale Russian reinforcements arrived from Europe. Trained by Prussian staff officers, Kodama regarded the railheads at

Lieutenant-General Kodama Gentaro, deputy chief of the IJA's general staff, began planning for war with Russia in October 1903. His basic strategy was focused on making the main effort in southern Manchuria to seize the Russian rail centre at Liaoyang, while only deploying secondary forces to capture or besiege Port Arthur. (Author's collection)

Liaoyang and Mukden as the enemy's operational-level centre of gravity.[17] Consequently, Kodama's broad-brush strategy emphasized landing two Japanese field armies in Korea and southern Manchuria, then rapidly pushing on to seize the railhead at Liaoyang. Given its small numerical edge, the IJA could not afford to divert too many troops on secondary missions, such as besieging Port Arthur. Without Liaoyang, the Russian military build-up in Manchuria would be seriously disrupted and give the IJA time to mobilize and deploy its own reserve formations. Kodama assessed that once Japan was able to deploy the bulk of its active and reserve divisions to Manchuria, it should be able to defend its territorial gains and exhaust any Russian counter-offensive – thereby leading to a negotiated peace. However, Kodama paid little attention to the Russian fleet or garrison in Port Arthur, assuming that both could be neutralized by blockade. Thus, the IJA's preferred course of action at Port Arthur was to leave that aspect of the campaign to the IJN, with minimal commitment of ground forces.

In contrast, the IJN was adamant about the need to neutralize the Russian Pacific Squadron at Port Arthur. Vice Admiral Ito Sukeyuki, chief of the naval general staff, and his deputy Vice Admiral Ijuin Goro, argued that once the Russian fleet was eliminated, the IJN would have complete naval superiority in the Far East. Thus, the navy regarded Port Arthur as the key to the entire war and wanted to take the leading role in neutralizing this position. Sukeyuki and Goro envisioned a surprise attack on the Russian fleet at Port Arthur, prior to a declaration of war, in order to inflict maximum damage on the enemy from the outset. However, the IJN general staff left detailed planning for naval operations against Port Arthur to Vice Admiral Togo Heihachiro, commander-in-chief of the Combined Fleet. Togo intended to deploy the bulk of his surface fleet to attack the Russian fleet in its anchorage. In order to support operations against Port Arthur, Togo directed the establishment of two advance bases in Korea – one near Mokpo on the south-west coast (600km from Port Arthur) and one near Masan on the southern coast. In December 1903, Togo took the Combined Fleet to the base near Masan and began intensively drilling the fleet in gunnery and torpedo exercises, in anticipation of imminent hostilities. Yet Togo's planning did not really extend beyond the initial blow and placed a great deal of faith in the Whitehead torpedoes acquired from Great Britain. Nor did Togo put much effort into developing a 'Plan B', in case the *coup de main* failed to cripple the enemy fleet. The idea of mining or blocking the harbour entrance was considered, but not regarded as necessary.

Thus, Japan went to war in February 1904 with the army and navy holding very different perceptions about how to deal with Port Arthur. It was not until Togo's Combined Fleet proved incapable of completely neutralizing the Russian fleet that the IJA was forced to develop plans for a siege and large-scale assault to capture Port Arthur. Thus, the Japanese campaign at Port Arthur would be an improvised affair, even though the whole point of going to war was to negate the base as a springboard for Russian power projection in East Asia.

---

17 According to the Prussian military theorist Karl von Clausewitz, the centre of gravity (COG) is the factor which enables the enemy to accomplish his campaign objectives. If the COG is negated, the enemy cannot prevail.

RUSSIAN

Imperial Russia began planning for war with Japan after the Triple Intervention in 1895. By that point, it was evident that Japan wanted not only the Liaodong Peninsula, but probably the rest of southern Manchuria as well – which was unacceptable to Russia's long-term strategic goals in the Far East. The main problem for Russian strategic planning was the tyranny of distance (over 8,000km by rail from St Petersburg to Manchuria), which made it difficult to deploy and sustain large ground armies in the Far East. The Trans-Siberian Railway was nearly completed, but it was still a single-track railway with very limited throughput. Whereas it had previously taken about 3–4 months to transfer a rifle corps from European Russia to Manchuria, the railway allowed a single corps to be transferred in about 2–3 weeks. Yet since there were no ammunition nor armaments factories in eastern Siberia, all munitions and equipment also had to be transported long distances, which reduced space for troops. Consequently, Russian strategy in the Far East was based on a 'hold–win' model, with the forces deployed in the region tasked with holding key positions until reinforcements arrived, enabling a general counter-offensive.

Russian contingency plans at the turn of the century assumed that six reserve rifle corps could be deployed to the Far East in four months after the declaration of war. The two key positions that had to be held were Port Arthur (as the primary base for the Russian Pacific Squadron) and the Liaoyang–Mukden section of the China Eastern Railway (CER). Liaoyang and Mukden would be the main staging area for the Russian reinforcements when they arrived. The Russian General Staff correctly assumed that the Japanese would land a corps-size force on the Liaodong Peninsula to isolate Port Arthur at the outset of a war – as they had in 1894 – so it was necessary to fortify the base to withstand a siege until a relief operation pushed down the CER. Initial planning made in 1898 for the fortification of the port was fairly grandiose, envisioning a strong

Russian strategy in the Far East was based upon the requirements of holding the main stations in southern Manchuria, in order to facilitate the transfer of larger forces from western Russia. Holding Port Arthur was not an essential element of that strategy. (Author's collection)

outer defence on land and powerful coastal forts. However, these plans languished for two years due to lack of funding and local resources. It was not until early 1900 that the General Staff sent Polkovnik Konstantin I. Velichko to Port Arthur to sketch out a plan for the fortification of the Liaodong Peninsula, which would henceforth be known as the Kwantung Fortified Area. Velichko was primarily an academic, not a field soldier, and he did not possess a good eye for key terrain. Consequently, the defensive lines he sketched out failed to take full advantage of the high ground overlooking the naval base and afforded very little depth to the defence. Actual construction work proceeded at a very slow pace, in part because funds kept getting diverted to other projects, but also due to the shortage of local skilled labour. Although other engineers estimated that it would require about 15 million rubles to properly fortify the region around Port Arthur, Velichko submitted a reduced-scale plan that was estimated to cost only 8.9 million rubles (about US $4.5 million). Nevertheless, only 4.6 million rubles was actually spent on fortifying Port Arthur between 1900 and 1903, and it was estimated that another five years would be required to complete the project. Six major forts were planned to protect the port's landward approaches, but only one was ready by 1904. Thus, the slow progress of the fortification effort at Port Arthur provided the Japanese with ample incentive to strike before the fortress was completed.

Another serious problem for the Russians in the defence of Port Arthur was the lack of serious planning between the army and navy on how to prevent the Japanese from isolating the Liaodong Peninsula in the first place. On paper, Vice Admiral Oskar Stark's Russian Pacific Squadron at Port Arthur, comprising seven battleships and six cruisers, had sufficient strength to intercept any Japanese landing operation within 150km of its main base. Yet Stark was risk-averse with his fleet because he knew that it would be almost impossible to repair any major battle damage to his ships in situ. Instead, he preferred to adopt a 'fleet in being' strategy, keeping his warships safe in or near Port Arthur, while relying on mines and coastal defences to whittle down the IJN. Unfortunately, this passive approach meant that the army garrison was expected to hold the naval base with little or no help from the fleet. Although the Russian Navy had pushed for the acquisition of Port Arthur, it was the Russian Army that was left with the difficult task of defending the base until a relief force could arrive.

The decision to hold Port Arthur also had a fateful impact upon all Russian operational planning in the Manchurian theatre. Not only was Kuropatkin forced to commit a full rifle corps to defend the port, but he had to commit another rifle corps to prepare for the expected relief operation. The commitment of such large resources into holding Port Arthur deprived Kuropatkin of any kind of operational flexibility. Rather than conserving his forces to hold Liaoyang until reinforcements provided him with an overwhelming superiority, Kuropatkin was forced to mount premature offensives and try to hold exposed positions for the sake of maintaining links with Port Arthur. Thus, a dilatory and flawed fortification effort at Port Arthur, combined with the lack of joint service planning and a theatre strategy that did not play to Russian strengths, set the stage for failure. Furthermore, the level of strategic emphasis placed upon holding Port Arthur meant that the damage to Russian national prestige if the base was lost would be grievous.

THE CAMPAIGN

OPENING MOVES

On 5 February 1904, Admiral Togo was informed that Japan was about to sever diplomatic relations with Russia and that he was to initiate hostilities soon afterwards. The next day, he sortied from Sasebo with his Combined Fleet, heading towards Port Arthur. Togo's basic plan, developed by the naval staff in Tokyo, was to conduct a surprise night attack with destroyers, then bombard the (hopefully) crippled Russian squadron at dawn with his battleships. However, Togo quickly began dispersing his strike force by sending one destroyer division to target Russian shipping near Dalny and another division to escort transports to land the advance guard of the First Army at Chemulpo (Incheon) in Korea. Consequently, only ten destroyers with a total capability to launch 20 45cm torpedoes were assigned to attack Vice Admiral Stark's squadron at Port Arthur.

At Port Arthur, Vice Admiral Stark was aware that hostilities with Japan might be approaching and had anchored his fleet in the roadstead outside the harbour (since it could take more than a day to sortie the entire fleet due to the shallow entrance) but under the protective guns of his coastal batteries. Stark also dispatched two Russian destroyers on picket duty and ordered his battleships to deploy their anti-torpedo nets. However, the coastal batteries were only half-manned and no mines had been laid around the harbour entrances. Unaware of these shortcomings, Stark was satisfied that he had

taken adequate defensive measures, and retired ashore with his staff on the evening of 8 February to attend a party. It was a cold, dark night and it was snowing, so visibility conditions were poor. Around 2100hrs, the approaching Japanese destroyers led by Captain Asai Shojiro bumped into the Russian picket vessels and became disorganized in their effort to evade them. It was not until 2345hrs that five Japanese destroyers (*Shirakumo, Asashio, Kasumi, Akatsuki* and *Ikazuchi*) approached the anchored Russian warships outside Port Arthur and launched seven 45cm torpedoes. Even at a range of a mere 600m against stationary targets, the

The Japanese destroyer *Kasumi* participated in the first surprise attack on the Russian squadron at Port Arthur on the night of 8/9 February 1904 and scored a torpedo hit on the cruiser *Pallada*. The *Kasumi* was built in Great Britain and was a modern warship, capable of making 30 knots and armed with torpedoes and quick-firing cannon. (Author's collection)

After being struck on the bow by a torpedo, the battleship *Retvizan* ran aground near the harbour entrance and was temporarily immobilized there for nearly a month. During this time, the *Retvizan* played a major role in defeating the first Japanese blockship operation. (Author's collection)

Japanese achieved just two hits: one on the bow of the battleship *Retvizan* and the other on the protected cruiser *Pallada*. The Russian fleet was thrown into confusion by the surprise attack, but was more alert when the other Japanese destroyers appeared around 0200hrs. This time, the Japanese were forced to launch their torpedoes from 1,500m and only achieved a single hit on the battleship *Tsesarevich*. Altogether, the Japanese destroyers fired 19 torpedoes in the surprise attack and achieved just three hits. Both *Retvizan* and the *Tsesarevich* suffered major damage, but were repairable.

Based upon the fragmentary reports he received from his destroyers, Togo apparently thought that the Russian fleet was badly hurt and disorganized, so he decided to risk a surface action with the Combined Fleet after sunrise. However, the Russian fleet recovered quickly from its initial shock and Togo proved rather slow in closing in on Port Arthur. This time, Togo's approaching fleet was spotted by a patrolling cruiser, enabling Stark to bring his fleet and coastal batteries up to full readiness. More than nine hours after the Japanese torpedo attack, Russian coastal batteries began engaging the approaching Combined Fleet. Togo's flagship *Mikasa* was hit by two 10in. shells from Battery No. 15 on Electric Hill, and soon both sides' warships were also firing away at each other. After an hour of sustained shooting, Togo decided to break off the action and retire. Although the four remaining Russian battleships were damaged by gunfire, four of Togo's battleships and three cruisers were also damaged. While the Japanese surprise naval attack on the Russian fleet at Port Arthur inflicted significant damage, it had failed to achieve the predicted knock-out blow, and Togo was now forced to shift to a distant blockade. Stark's command performance was mediocre but he still managed to rally his command while under attack and see off Togo's bombardment squadron. Nevertheless, the Tsar decided to immediately relieve Stark of command and send the more energetic Vice Admiral Stepan Makarov from St Petersburg to take command of the Pacific Squadron.

The five 10in. guns of Battery No. 15 on Electric Cliff played a major role in driving off Togo's fleet on the morning of 19 February 1904. The guns were set in concrete emplacements, and the crews were protected by armoured canopies. (Author's collection)

Alekseyev over-reacted to the Japanese attack and declared that the fortress was under a state of siege, even though Togo's fleet had withdrawn and no Japanese troops had yet landed. The result was a panic, that led to thousands of Chinese labourers fleeing the city as well as civilian freighters, some of which carried foodstuffs or other useful cargoes. Alekseyev ordered General-leytenant Anatoli M. Stoessel to bring the 22,500-man garrison up to full readiness in anticipation of a Japanese landing somewhere on the Liaodong Peninsula. Small company-size scouting detachments were sent to monitor likely landing sites along the coast, and Polkovnik Nikolai A. Tretyakov's 5th East Siberian Rifle Regiment was sent to occupy a blocking position at Nanshan Hill, some 50km north-east of Port Arthur. Nanshan Hill appeared to offer an excellent defensive position, with high ground dominating a narrow isthmus, but the 8km-wide front was far too much for a single regiment to hold. General-mayor Aleksandr V. Fok's 4th East Siberian Rifle Division was placed nearby in reserve, but Fok refused to provide Tretyakov with any additional troops. On the one hand, Alekseyev wanted Stoessel to defend the commercial port at Dalny (which had seen considerable Russian commercial investment) but on the other he did not want to risk too many troops defending Nanshan Hill.

The Japanese tried repeatedly to block the entrance to Port Arthur's inner harbour with blockship operations, all of which failed. Here, wrecks of Japanese steamers litter the coast near the entrance. (Author's collection)

Two days after the attack, Alekseyev ordered Stark to begin laying mines in the waters around Port Arthur. Both Amur-class minelayers were sent out on the morning of 11 February to lay minefields, but the operation quickly turned into a fiasco. The minelayer *Yeneisei* accidentally drifted into one of its own mines and sank with heavy loss of life, then its escort, the protected cruiser *Boyarin*, also struck one of the Russian mines and was lost. After these losses, Stark became even more averse to risking his warships. Togo was less reticent but he preferred to neutralize the Russian Pacific Squadron at the lowest possible cost, so he decided to attempt a special operation. Before the war, two Japanese naval officers had developed a plan to block the narrow entrance to Port Arthur's harbour with a flotilla of blockships. Five obsolete civilian steamships were chosen for the mission, manned by 77 volunteers. On the night of 23/24 February, the five blockships, escorted by four destroyers, quietly approached the entrance to Port Arthur. Apparently Togo did not realize that the damaged battleship *Retvizan* was still grounded near the harbour entrance, and the blockships headed straight for this warship. Around 0415hrs, the Russian coastal defences spotted the unknown vessels and illuminated them with searchlights, then opened fire. The battleship *Retvizan* joined in, smashing the flimsy freighters with point-blank fire. Gunfire sank four of the blockships and the fifth ran into the Russian minefield and blew up. Togo's first blockship operation was a failure. Following this raid, Togo appeared off Port Arthur on the morning of 24 February, in order to ascertain the outcome of the raid – which demonstrates how poor Togo's situational awareness was about the status of the port and the Russian squadron.

From February until early May, the garrison in Port Arthur retained both rail and telegraphic links with Kuropatkin's headquarters in Liaoyang. On 7 March, guns, ammunition and reservists from European Russia arrived in Port Arthur to reinforce the garrison. The next day, Admiral Makarov arrived with a large team of naval engineers to begin repairs on the two damaged battleships. Makarov immediately adopted a more aggressive approach with the fleet, in order to build up morale and combat effectiveness. While Makarov was busy restoring the fleet, Togo came up with another means of striking at the Russian warships inside the harbour. In order to

Three Petropavlovsk-class battleships with the Russian Pacific Squadron in Port Arthur. Although the squadron had the capability to contest the Japanese landing on the Liaodong Peninsula, the Russian naval leadership preferred not to risk its capital ships in a fleet action. (Author's collection)

avoid the Russian coastal batteries, on 10 March Togo sent the battleships *Fuji* and *Yashima* to bombard the port from Pigeon Bay, on the west side of the peninsula. Even though the bombardment was conducted without benefit of observers to correct the fall of shot, incredibly the Japanese scored two lucky hits on the *Retvizan* and *Tsesarevich*, which further delayed their repairs. In response, Makarov moved four 6in. naval guns to cover Pigeon Bay and established observer positions with telephone links to the fleet in Port Arthur. When Togo repeated this tactic on 22 March, this time the Japanese were caught by surprise and *Retvizan* managed to score a hit on the *Fuji*, causing the Japanese warships to withdraw. In the history of naval warfare, this was probably the only action where two opposing battleship squadrons engaged each other with a significant landmass in between. On 27 March, Togo attempted his second blockship operation with four more civilian steamers, but Makarov had the fleet on high alert and had deployed destroyers and gunboats near the harbour mouth. When the four Japanese steamers appeared, they were quickly spotted and sunk.

General-leytenant Konstantin Smirnov arrived in Port Arthur on 17 March, with orders from Alekseyev to replace Stoessel. However, Stoessel took advantage of the vagueness in Alekseyev's orders and opted to ignore Smirnov and remain in effective command of the entire Kwantung Fortified Area. Even worse, Alekseyev finally concluded that Port Arthur was not under siege and that some of garrison might be better utilized elsewhere. Consequently, during March over 5,000 troops were transferred from Port Arthur – nearly 20 per cent of the garrison – in order to create a covering force on the Yalu River. The Japanese First Army was moving rapidly north through Korea, and Alekseyev created an ad hoc corps-size formation known as the Eastern Detachment to delay their crossing of the Yalu River. Amazingly, Alekseyev's orders stripped the Port Arthur garrison of all its sappers and signal troops, which seriously impeded efforts to improve the defensive perimeter and establish communication links to key positions. Likewise, Tretyakov was denied the troops and basic resources (such as picks and shovels) he needed to fully fortify the blocking position at Nanshan Hill. Alekseyev also ordered the fleet to dismount dozens of guns with crews to augment the land defences, but this seriously reduced the fighting capabilities of the warships.

With the IJA preparing to land troops on the Liaodong Peninsula, Togo was under pressure to seek new methods of neutralizing Makarov's Pacific

Squadron. Another civilian steamer was hastily converted into a minelayer. On the night of 12/13 April, the minelayer was escorted by four destroyers and laid 48 contact mines about 5km south-east of Port Arthur. At dawn on 13 April, the Russian destroyer *Strashny* went to investigate the suspicious activity, but blundered into the Japanese escort vessels and was quickly sunk. In response, the armoured cruiser *Bayan* went to rescue survivors, but retreated after finding that two Japanese cruisers had arrived to reinforce their destroyer flotilla. Makarov observed these skirmishes and decided to immediately sortie at 0700hrs with the battleships *Petropavlovsk* and *Poltava* plus three more cruisers to engage the Japanese cruiser–destroyer force, with the rest of the fleet to follow. However, when Makarov sighted Togo's main fleet approaching, he decided to reverse course. By one of the unpredictable hazards of war, the *Petropavlovsk* struck one of the contact mines at 0942hrs, which caused a catastrophic explosion in the forward magazine; the battleship broke in half and sank in two minutes. Makarov and 678 Russian sailors were killed in the disaster, which shattered morale in the Pacific Fleet. The battleship *Pobeda* also hit a mine, but made it back to port.

Shortly after Makarov's death, Alekseyev returned to Port Arthur with some of his staff. He decided to put one of his staff cronies, Rear Admiral Vilgelm K. Vitgeft, in charge of the Pacific Squadron. Vitgeft was unable to restore morale among the crews, and his adoption of the passive 'fleet-in-being' approach effectively ceded local naval superiority to Togo. Meanwhile, General Kuroki's First Army was advancing rapidly through Korea, and Lieutenant-General Kodama now judged that the time was approaching to land General Oku's Second Army on the Liaodong Peninsula. However, the IJA leadership was reluctant to land so close to Port Arthur when the Russian Pacific Squadron was still capable of conducting a sortie to strike the troop transports. Consequently, Togo was enjoined to mount another blockship operation. By this point, Togo had established a forward operating base in the Elliot Islands (modern Guangludao), just 110km north-east of Port Arthur. Trusting to mass rather than stealth, Togo assembled a dozen civilian steamers and over 270 volunteers for the operation, led by a veteran sailor, Lieutenant-Commander Hayashi Mineo. The operation began on the night of 2/3 May, but Mineo decided to abort the attempt due to deteriorating weather conditions. However, eight of the 12 steamers did not see his signal and continued on towards Port Arthur. Once again, the slow-moving Japanese steamers, loaded with concrete, were spotted by the searchlights as they moved towards the narrow harbour entrance. One by one, the steamers were destroyed and none got within 500m of their goal. All eight steamers and 115 crewmen were lost. Despite this failure, Togo decided to lie to his superiors and reported that the raid was a success, so that the landing of General Oku's Second

On 13 April 1904, Vice Admiral Makarov's flagship, the battleship *Petropavlovsk*, struck a mine off Port Arthur and sank within two minutes. The death of Makarov left the Russian Pacific Squadron demoralized just prior to the Japanese amphibious landing on the Liaodong Peninsula. (Author's collection)

JAPANESE NAVAL ATTACKS ON PORT ARTHUR, FEBRUARY–APRIL 1904

Admiral Togo made repeated efforts to cripple the Russian fleet in Port Arthur, using all the weapons available to him, but failed to permanently neutralize the enemy battleships. The Russian naval strategy of hiding behind their mines and coastal batteries proved frustrating for the IJN's aggressive leadership, which could not come to grips with their enemy.

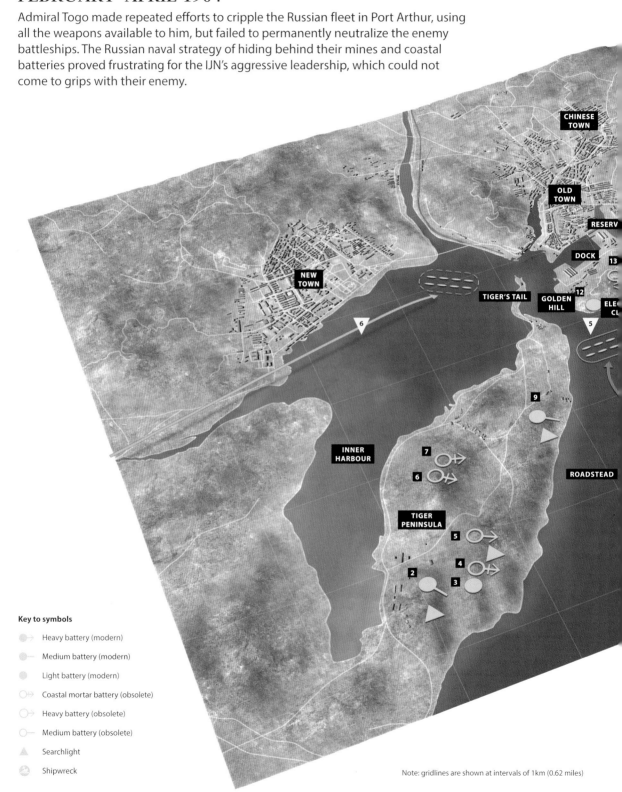

CHINESE TOWN

OLD TOWN

RESERV

DOCK

13

NEW TOWN

TIGER'S TAIL

GOLDEN HILL

12

ELE CL

5

6

9

INNER HARBOUR

7

6

ROADSTEAD

TIGER PENINSULA

5

4

2

3

Key to symbols

- Heavy battery (modern)
- Medium battery (modern)
- Light battery (modern)
- Coastal mortar battery (obsolete)
- Heavy battery (obsolete)
- Medium battery (obsolete)
- Searchlight
- Shipwreck

Note: gridlines are shown at intervals of 1km (0.62 miles)

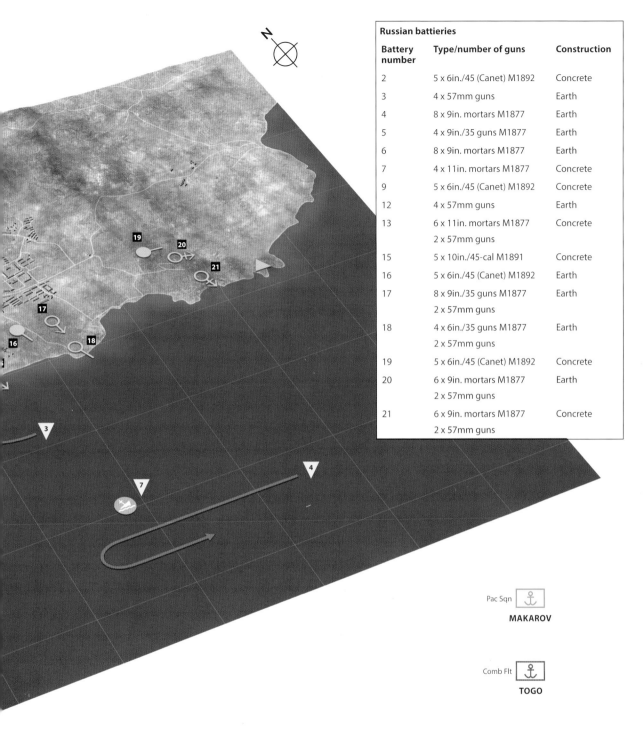

Russian battieries		
Battery number	**Type/number of guns**	**Construction**
2	5 x 6in./45 (Canet) M1892	Concrete
3	4 x 57mm guns	Earth
4	8 x 9in. mortars M1877	Earth
5	4 x 9in./35 guns M1877	Earth
6	8 x 9in. mortars M1877	Earth
7	4 x 11in. mortars M1877	Concrete
9	5 x 6in./45 (Canet) M1892	Concrete
12	4 x 57mm guns	Earth
13	6 x 11in. mortars M1877 2 x 57mm guns	Concrete
15	5 x 10in./45-cal M1891	Concrete
16	5 x 6in./45 (Canet) M1892	Earth
17	8 x 9in./35 guns M1877 2 x 57mm guns	Earth
18	4 x 6in./35 guns M1877 2 x 57mm guns	Earth
19	5 x 6in./45 (Canet) M1892	Concrete
20	6 x 9in. mortars M1877 2 x 57mm guns	Earth
21	6 x 9in. mortars M1877 2 x 57mm guns	Concrete

Pac Sqn **MAKAROV**

Comb Flt **TOGO**

EVENTS

1. 8 February 1904: Russian fleet anchored in line off Golden Hill.

2. 8 February, 2345hrs: first Japanese torpedo attack.

3. 9 February, 0200hrs: second Japanese torpedo attack.

4. 9 February, 1100hrs: Togo conducts a bombardment of the Russian fleet, then withdraws.

5. 24 February, 27 March and 3 May: three attempts are made to obstruct the harbour entrance with blockships – all of which fail.

6. 10 and 22 March: the Japanese battleships *Fuji* and *Yashima* bombard Port Arthur from Pigeon Bay, scoring several lucky hits on the Russian fleet in the inner harbour.

7. 13 April: Makarov's flagship, the battleship *Petropavlovsk*, is sunk off the harbour entrance by Japanese mines.

The Japanese Second Army began its landing operation on the Liaodong Peninsula on 5 May 1904. The army and navy used a motley collection of sampans and fishing boats to land troops directly onto the beach. Until the capture of Dalny, Japanese logistics in the Liaodong Peninsula were precarious. (Author's collection)

Russian naval contact mines on the shore near the entrance to Port Arthur, with sunk blockships in the background. Although their design was nearly 50 years old, they proved quite effective in combat. (Author's collection)

Army would proceed as planned. When Kodama learned that Kuroki's First Army had defeated Zasulitch's Eastern detachment on the Yalu, he ordered Oku's Second Army to begin its landing operation.

The Japanese amphibious landing on the Liaodong Peninsula did not begin under auspicious conditions. The beach chosen near Pit-zu-wo (modern Pikouzhen/Laolongtou) was rocky, and weather conditions were poor. Nevertheless, around 0630hrs on 5 May, a battalion of naval infantry began disembarking onto the rocky coastline to secure the beach. Soon thereafter, a battalion from the 3rd Infantry Division began landing – the vanguard of Oku's Second Army. A Russian mounted detachment from the 1st Verkhneudinsky Cossack Regiment observed the landing, but quickly left to report the news to General Fok, who was responsible for coastal security in this sector. Fok made no effort to interfere with the Japanese landing, even though he had more than enough troops nearby to mount a serious counter-attack against a single battalion. Likewise, Vitgeft did not dispatch a single warship to attack the Japanese transport fleet, which lay just 115km from Port Arthur. While it is probable that Togo's Combined Fleet could have repulsed a Russian naval sortie, even a modest effort might have delayed Oku's landing. Instead, Oku's Second Army was allowed to land unmolested and to consolidate its beachhead, although it took ten days to land all three divisions. It was not until 10 May that Oku began to move some scout detachments 30km westwards to interfere with Russian rail traffic, and even then one last ammunition train made it through to Port Arthur. Reports of trains being fired upon 40km north of Nanshan spurred Fok into mounting a reconnaissance in force, using a large portion of his division and two-thirds of Treyakov's regiment. The Russian advance between 11 and 15 May was sluggish and only proceeded 15km before bumping into a few Japanese scouts; although Fok enjoyed a large numerical superiority, he ordered his division to fall back to Nanshan after brief skirmishing.

Despite Vitgeft's inactivity, Togo was still concerned that the Russians would try to interfere with the landing of Oku's army, so he decided to shift to a close blockade of Port Arthur during the period of maximum vulnerability. On the morning of 15 May, Togo sent three battleships and four cruisers to reinforce the patrols off Port Arthur. Before dawn, the armoured cruiser *Kasuga* collided with the protected cruiser *Yoshino* in a heavy fog; the *Yoshino* sank with the loss of 319 sailors. The Japanese

Advance of the Japanese Third Army towards Port Arthur, 30 May–31 July 1904

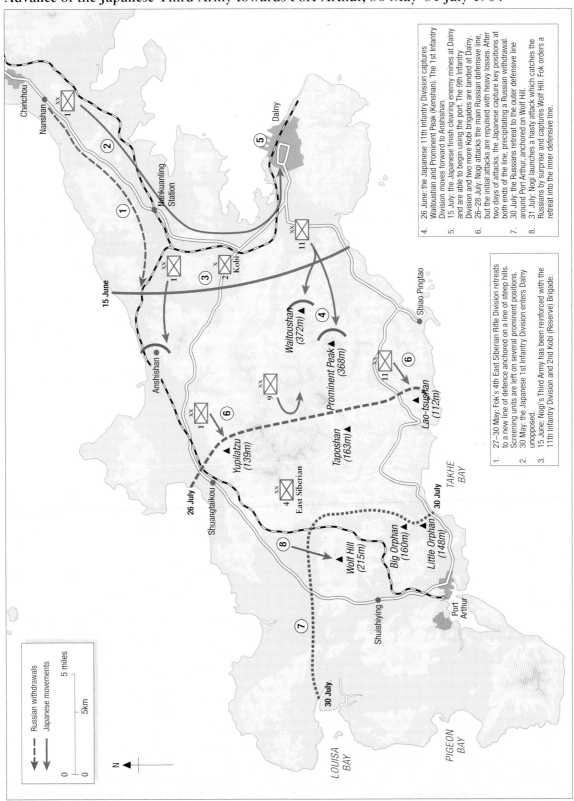

1. 27–30 May: Fok's 4th East Siberian Rifle Division retreats to a new line of defence anchored on a line of steep hills. Screening units are left on several prominent positions. 30 May: the Japanese 1st Infantry Division enters Dalny unopposed.

2. 15 June: Nogi's Third Army has been reinforced with the 11th Infantry Division and 2nd Kobi (Reserve) Brigade.

3. 15 June: Nogi's Third Army has been reinforced with the 11th Infantry Division and 2nd Kobi (Reserve) Brigade.

4. 26 June: the Japanese 11th Infantry Division captures Waitoushan and Prominent Peak (Kenshan). The 1st Infantry Division moves forward to Anshishan.

5. 15 July: the Japanese finish clearing enemy mines at Dalny and are able to begin using the port. The 9th Infantry Division and two more Kobi brigades are landed at Dalny.

6. 26–28 July: Nogi attacks the main Russian defensive line, but the initial attacks are repulsed with heavy losses. After two days of attacks, the Japanese capture key positions at both ends of the line, precipitating a Russian withdrawal.

7. 30 July: the Russians retreat to the outer defensive line around Port Arthur, anchored on Wolf Hill.

8. 31 July: Nogi launches a hasty attack which catches the Russians by surprise and captures Wolf Hill. Fok orders a retreat into the inner defensive line.

Russian withdrawals
Japanese movements

5 miles
5km

Chinchou
Nanshan
Nankuanling Station
Dalny
15 June
Anshishan
Kobi
Waitoushan (372m)
Prominent Peak (368m)
Shiao Pingtao
Lao-tsushan (112m)
Yupilatzu (139m)
Taposhan (163m)
26 July
Shuangtaikou
East Siberian
TAKHE BAY
30 July
Wolf Hill (215m)
Big Orphan (160m)
Little Orphan (148m)
Shuishiying
Port Arthur
30 July
LOUISA BAY
PIGEON BAY

39

On the morning of 15 May 1904, the Japanese battleship *Hatsuse* sank after hitting a mine. Shortly afterwards, the battleship *Yashima* was also mortally damaged by a mine. The loss of one-third of Togo's battleships on one day threatened the Japanese ability to control the sea around Port Arthur. (Author's collection)

Polkovnik Nikolai A. Tretyakov, commander of the 5th East Siberian Rifle Regiment. Although only a mid-level officer, Tretyakov played a major role in the Battle of Nanshan and the defence of 203-metre Hill. As a trained engineer officer, Tretyakov excelled in creating formidable defensive positions. (Author's collection)

squadron continued on to Port Arthur and the fog cleared. Unaware that the Russians had begun to lay mines further out, the Japanese steamed straight into a newly laid minefield. Around 1110hrs, the battleship *Hatsuse* hit two mines and sank in less than a minute, with 495 of her crew. Shortly thereafter, the battleship *Yashima* also hit a mine, but was able to get out of view of Port Arthur before sinking. The day had been a disaster for the IJN – Togo had lost two of his six battleships and a cruiser, along with 814 sailors. After this incident, Togo was forced to pull his remaining heavy warships off blockade duty, which enabled some blockade runners to slip in and out of Port Arthur.

FIGHT FOR THE OUTER PERIMETER

Initially, Oku moved only one infantry division south down the rail line towards Nanshan, while keeping the rest of the Second Army oriented northwards, in case Kuropatkin decided to send reinforcements to re-establish rail communications with Port Arthur. Japanese scouts soon made Oku aware of the Russian blocking position at Nanshan, and once he had the last of his troops ashore, he began preparing for an attack south. In Port Arthur, Stoessel was nominally in charge, but he issued no real orders beyond vague and often contradictory guidance. Fok was told to hold Kinchou (modern Jinzhou), even though it was north of the Nanshan position. He was also ordered to assign troops and artillery to protect the commercial port of Dalny, 18km south of Nanshan. Consequently, Fok directed Tretyakov to keep several infantry companies and an artillery battery deployed forward to hold an exposed outpost line, even though the main position on Nanshan Hill was not fully manned. Furthermore, Fok ignored Tretyakov's requests for reinforcements and kept six battalions of the 4th East

Siberian Rifle Division near Dalny, to protect it from a potential amphibious landing.

On the night of 18/19 May, the Japanese began pushing in Tretyakov's outposts, inflicting heavy casualties on one of his rifle companies. Tretyakov ordered his outposts to pull back into the environs of Kinchou, which was protected by a 3m-high Chinese wall. The Japanese 4th Infantry Division made several attacks on Kinchou over the next few days, but had difficulty breaching the thick walls. Stoessel visited the forward positions on 21 May and criticized Tretyakov for pulling back his outposts – but offered token artillery reinforcements, including a single 6in. naval gun. By the night of 25/26 May, it was obvious that Oku's Second Army was massing for a major assault, so Tretyakov ordered his 400

A Chinese civilian sits on Tretyakov's command post atop Nanshan Hill, looking south towards Talien Bay. Notice the use of sandbags on the parapet and boxes to create fire steps. The Russian position at Nanshan was well sited and effectively blocked the narrow neck of the Liaodong Peninsula. (Author's collection)

troops in Kinchou to evacuate the town and withdraw to the main defensive position. Before dawn on 26 May, the Japanese infantry moved into the deserted streets of Kinchou.

Oku arrayed his Second Army in a broad semi-circle around Nanshan, with Lieutenant-General Ogawa Mataji's 4th Infantry Division on his right flank, Imperial Prince Fushimi Sadanaru's 1st Infantry Division in the centre and Lieutenant-General Oshima Yoshimasa's 3rd Infantry Division on his left flank. The 1st Artillery Brigade provided additional firepower. Altogether, the Second Army deployed 34 infantry battalions (with about 30,000 infantry), supported by 216 guns (mostly 75mm). In addition, the IJN would support the attack with four gunboats (mounting a total of 24 guns), deployed on the west side of the peninsula. Tretyakov had three infantry battalions with about 2,700 troops to defend Nanshan Hill, supported by 69 guns (including 36 87mm M1877 field guns and 13 106mm siege guns) and ten machine guns. The Russian infantry were well dug-in behind barbed-wire obstacles and landmines – the first time that this type of defence had been employed in a major battle. However, Tretyakov had only a single company in reserve and his supporting artillery had very limited ammunition. On paper, the Japanese enjoyed a 12:1 numerical superiority over Tretyakov's regiment.

At 0520hrs on 26 May, Oku's army began a three-hour artillery preparation with over 200 guns, which was expected to suppress the Russian defences. However, most of the Japanese shells were 75mm shrapnel rounds, which had little effect upon the well-built Russian redoubts. Around 0600hrs, four Japanese gunboats appeared off the western shore and began engaging the Russian positions with an annoying enfilade fire, which did inflict some damage and casualties. Unwisely, the Russian artillery tried to match the Japanese artillery bombardment – but this only served to rapidly deplete their limited stock of ammunition. After three hours of pounding away at the Russian positions, Oku noted that the Russian artillery fire was dropping off so he decided it was time to commit his infantry. He opted to make his main effort on his left, with Oshima's 3rd Infantry Division, while Prince Fushimi's 1st Infantry Division made a supporting attack in the centre. Around 0830hrs, the Japanese infantry moved forwards in dense skirmish-line formations but were abruptly stopped about 300–400m from

THE BATTLE OF NANSHAN HILL, 26 MAY 1904

The Japanese Second Army launched a major assault with three divisions against the Russian blocking position on Nanshan Hill, held by Tretyakov's 5th East Siberian Rifle Regiment. This was the first major battle in which a modern army attacked a position defended by barbed-wire obstacles and machine guns, which inflicted heavy losses on the Japanese.

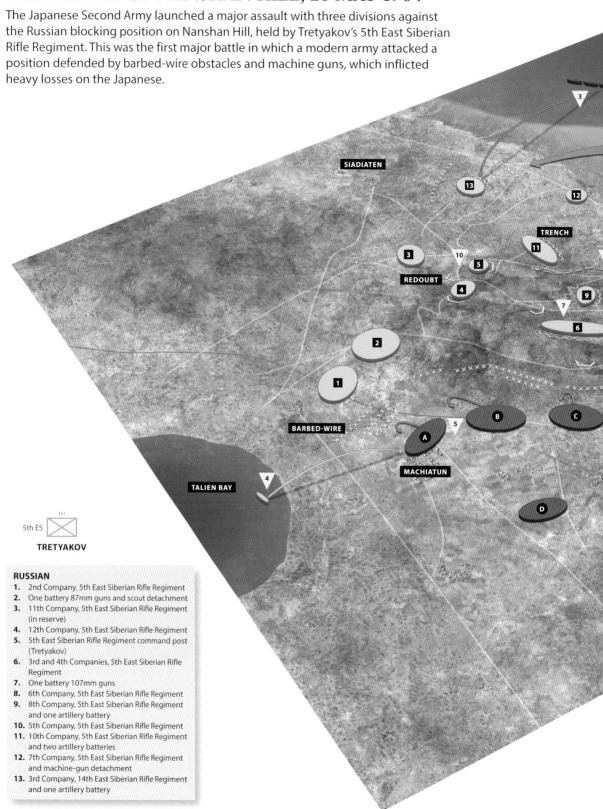

5th ES

TRETYAKOV

RUSSIAN
1. 2nd Company, 5th East Siberian Rifle Regiment
2. One battery 87mm guns and scout detachment
3. 11th Company, 5th East Siberian Rifle Regiment (in reserve)
4. 12th Company, 5th East Siberian Rifle Regiment
5. 5th East Siberian Rifle Regiment command post (Tretyakov)
6. 3rd and 4th Companies, 5th East Siberian Rifle Regiment
7. One battery 107mm guns
8. 6th Company, 5th East Siberian Rifle Regiment
9. 8th Company, 5th East Siberian Rifle Regiment and one artillery battery
10. 5th Company, 5th East Siberian Rifle Regiment
11. 10th Company, 5th East Siberian Rifle Regiment and two artillery batteries
12. 7th Company, 5th East Siberian Rifle Regiment and machine-gun detachment
13. 3rd Company, 14th East Siberian Rifle Regiment and one artillery battery

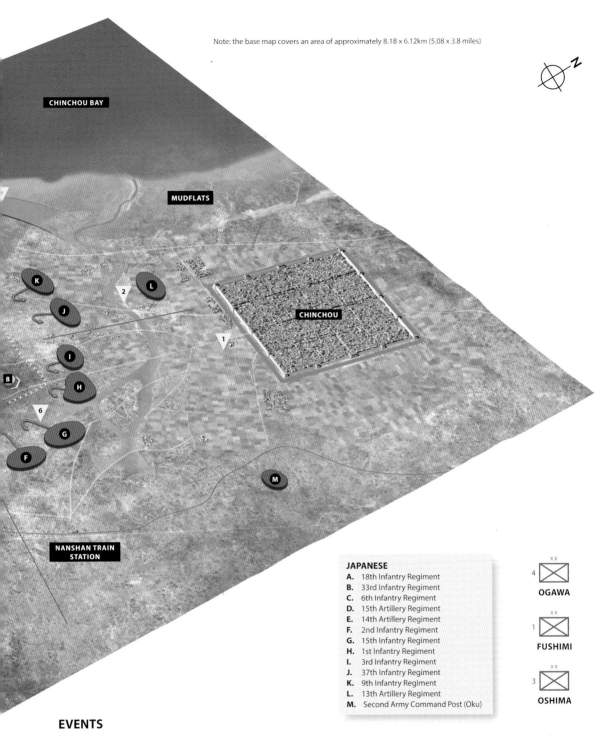

Note: the base map covers an area of approximately 8.18 x 6.12km (5.08 x 3.8 miles)

N

CHINCHOU BAY

MUDFLATS

CHINCHOU

NANSHAN TRAIN
STATION

JAPANESE

A. 18th Infantry Regiment
B. 33rd Infantry Regiment
C. 6th Infantry Regiment
D. 15th Artillery Regiment
E. 14th Artillery Regiment
F. 2nd Infantry Regiment
G. 15th Infantry Regiment
H. 1st Infantry Regiment
I. 3rd Infantry Regiment
J. 37th Infantry Regiment
K. 9th Infantry Regiment
L. 13th Artillery Regiment
M. Second Army Command Post (Oku)

4 ⊠ OGAWA

1 ⊠ FUSHIMI

3 ⊠ OSHIMA

EVENTS

26 May 1904

1. 0300hrs: The Russian rear-guard evacuates Chinchou before it is surrounded by the advancing Japanese.

2. 0520hrs: The Japanese Second Army begins a three-hour artillery preparation against the main Russian positions on Nanshan Hill.

3. 0600hrs: Four Japanese warships arrive and eventually knock out all the Russian guns in Battery No. 15.

4. 0800hrs: The Russian gunboat *Bobr* arrives and provides fire support for about an hour.

5. 0830hrs: The Japanese begin their ground assault, making the main effort on the left with the 3rd Infantry Division. Japanese infantry try to use the village of Machiatun for cover to approach the Russian lines, but are stopped.

6. 0830hrs: The Japanese 1st Infantry Division makes a strong attack in the centre, which is repulsed with heavy losses.

7. 1200hrs: All Russian artillery ammunition has been expended.

8. 1600hrs: The 5th Company begins to retire in disorder after suffering from heavy bombardment.

9. 1800hrs: The Japanese 4th Infantry Division mounts a flank attack through the surf and succeeds in dislodging Tretyakov's left flank.

10. Tretyakov tries to mount a counter-attack, but Fok orders a withdrawal.

A Russian Maxim machine gun on a wheeled mount, with an armoured shield. Note that the gunner is sitting and that the weapon has no traverse capability, which means that it can only fire along a fixed axis. (Author's collection)

the Russian positions when they encountered three rows of barbed wire. The Japanese infantry had not been trained to breach this type of obstacle and lacked wirecutters. Halted by the wire, the Japanese infantry became perfect targets for the Maxim machine gunners on the hilltop as well as the entrenched Russian infantry. Consequently, the first wave of attackers was decimated and succeeding waves sought cover and were pinned down. The Russian gunboat *Bobr* appeared in Talien Bay and poured flanking fire into the 3rd Infantry Division, further adding to the Japanese discomfiture.

Oku ordered more attacks, but casualties quickly mounted and no progress was made over the next six hours. The few Japanese troops who managed to slip through the barbed wire encountered fougasse and anti-personnel mines, which provided another shock. Oku was baffled by the inability of his infantry to advance and simply kept issuing orders to continue with more of the same tactics. Despite the best efforts of Japanese officers to exhort their troops, the infantry was repulsed time and again with heavy casualties. However, the Russian artillery had exhausted their ammunition by 1200hrs and the Japanese artillery focused on a few positions, which caused the battered 5th Company, 5th East Siberian Rifle Regiment to withdraw without permission. By this point, Japanese naval gunfire had also silenced some of the Russian redoubts on the left flank, which created an opening. Around 1530hrs, Ogawa's 4th Infantry Division made a risky effort to outflank the Russian positions by sending its 9th Infantry Regiment across the open mudflats. Russian machine guns, manned by sailors, ripped into these exposed troops, but on this occasion the fanaticism of the attacking infantry prevailed. By 1600hrs, Ogawa's troops had outflanked the Russian positions and Tretyakov's left flank began to unravel, as the 7th Company also pulled back. Tretyakov appealed to Fok for reinforcements to restore his line. At first Fok promised two infantry companies, but then changed his mind and ordered a withdrawal without informing Tretyakov. The result was a disorganized retreat from Nanshan Hill, which abandoned all crew-served weapons. During the course of the day, Tretyakov's regiment had suffered only light losses, but he lost over 600 men in the pell-mell retreat. Altogether, Tretyakov's 5th East Siberian Rifle Regiment suffered 1,616 casualties (including 182 killed and 598 missing) and lost ten machine guns and 82 artillery pieces.

From the Japanese point of view, the Battle of Nanshan was a shocking event. Despite its large superiority in manpower and firepower, Oku's

Second Army had been stymied for eight hours and suffered over 10 per cent casualties. Sources disagree on Japanese losses, with the total number being between 4,200 and 6,200, including 683–749 dead. The Japanese infantry expended 2.2 million rounds of small-arms ammunition (half just by the 4th Infantry Division) but hit very little. Japanese artillerymen played a large part in the costly victory, but expended 34,000 rounds or 79 per cent of their on-hand ammunition. Oku's bruised Second Army had lost the equivalent of six battalions and consumed most of its ammunition, forcing it to halt operations for several days. In Japan, the War Ministry was shocked by the expenditure of lives and ammunition in what was supposed to be a secondary operation. Foreign military observers noted the role played by barbed wire, trenches and machine guns in levelling the playing field, but regarded the action as something of a fluke.

After withdrawing from Nanshan, Fok's 4th East Siberian Rifle Division withdrew 30km to the west, to a new line established on the 'Green Hills'. The commercial port of Dalny was evacuated, but the waters around it were heavily mined. Oku sent the 1st Infantry Division to occupy Dalny and keep an eye on Fok's division, but pivoted the rest of the Second Army to face northwards towards Liaoyang. In Port Arthur, Stoessel was shocked by the sudden evacuation of Nanshan (although he had done nothing to reinforce this key position) and appealed to the theatre commander, Alekseyev, for immediate reinforcements (Stoessel regularly sent dispatches to Yingkou via blockade runners). Kuropatkin was opposed to detaching forces to try to relieve Port Arthur since it undermined his long-term strategy of amassing a large force for the decisive battle around Liaoyang, but he had to yield to *force majeure* when the Tsar became involved. Reluctantly, Kuropatkin ordered General-leytenant Georg von Stackelberg's 1st Siberian Rifle Corps to advance down the rail line towards Port Arthur and reoccupy Nanshan if feasible. This was not a token effort – von Stackelberg was given the equivalent of 2½ rifle divisions and provided with some of the new 76.2mm M1903 Putilov field guns. Von Stackelberg advanced in bounds down the rail line, before encountering Oku's Second Army at Te-li-Ssu, 83km north of Nanshan, on 14 June. Oku enjoyed numerical superiority in men and guns, but the real difference was that the Japanese were allowed to fight the kind of free-wheeling manoeuvre battle that quickly put von Stackelberg's corps at risk of being outflanked. After suffering 3,500 casualties, von Stackelberg opted to withdraw, thus ending the one Russian attempt to reopen communications with the Port Arthur garrison. After the failure of the relief effort, Kuropatkin tried to relieve Stoessel of command by ordering him out of the Liaodong Peninsula, but Stoessel claimed that it was too risky for him to leave on a blockade runner.

On 6 June, General Nogi Maresuke arrived on the Liaodong Peninsula to activate the Third Army. At this point,

A battery of Russian 76mm field guns dug into firing pits atop a hill. Initially, the Russians sought to fight a protracted covering-force battle on the high ground east of Port Arthur, in order to delay the Japanese Third Army from investing the port itself. (Author's collection)

RUSSIAN MACHINE GUNS IN ACTION AT NANSHAN HILL, 26 MAY 1904 (PP. 46–47)

Polkovnik Nikolai A. Tretyakov's 5th East Siberian Rifle Regiment had been fortifying the blocking position at Nanshan Hill since mid-February 1904. Over the course of three months, Tretyakov's soldiers (with the enforced assistance of Chinese civilians) dug trenches, emplaced barbed-wire obstacles and laid land mines. Tretyakov's regiment was also provided with 67 artillery pieces and ten Maxim machine guns to augment its defensive firepower. On the night of 25/26 May, General Oku Yasukata's Second Army began pushing in Tretyakov's combat outposts, and prepared to mount a full-scale assault with all three infantry divisions the next morning. On paper, the Japanese enjoyed a 12:1 numerical superiority over Tretyakov's regiment. At 0520hrs on 26 May, Oku's army began a three-hour artillery preparation from over 200 guns, which was expected to suppress the Russian defences. Around 0830hrs, Prince Fushimi Sadanaru's 1st Infantry Division deployed to attack the Russian right flank with its 1st and 15th Infantry regiments on line.

Since the Russian artillery had already expended most of its ammunition, the Japanese infantry initially suffered few casualties as they advanced on-line towards the Russian hilltop positions. However, Japanese troops had never encountered barbed-wire obstacles before and their artillery preparation had failed to suppress the Russian defences. Lacking wire cutters or clear direction on how to get through the obstacle, the Japanese advance hesitated, about 300 yards from the Russian trenches, but fully inside the engagement area of the Russian Maxim machine-gun battery defending Tretyakov's right flank.

Here, the Russian Maxim battery (**1**), supported by riflemen from the 3rd Company (**2**) in the forward trenches, is engaging Japanese infantry from the 15th Infantry Regiment. The Japanese troops are hung up on the barbed wire (**3**) and taking heavy casualties. Russian land mines (**4**) are detonating, further disrupting the attackers. Despite the efforts of Japanese officers, many of their infantry are seeking cover or falling back in confusion.

Over the course of the next seven hours, Prince Fushimi's division would mount further assaults, but each was repulsed in turn. By late afternoon, the Japanese 1st Infantry Division had suffered 1,359 casualties – roughly 10 per cent of the troops engaged – without ever reaching the Russian trench line. Eventually, the Japanese 4th Infantry Division succeeded in turning Tretyakov's left flank, which led to a withdrawal. Nevertheless, the Battle at Nanshan was the first time that the IJA encountered a well-prepared defence, based upon machine guns and barbed wire, which demonstrated that an offensive doctrine based on élan was insufficient on the modern battlefield.

the 1st Infantry Division was transferred to his command, but since he had no other combat units available he could not immediately advance towards Port Arthur. By 15 June, the 11th Infantry Division and the 2nd Kobi (Reserve) Brigade had arrived, although Japanese logistics were meagre because the port of Dalny was still closed by Russian mines (it took the IJN six weeks to clear all these). As a result, nearly a month passed with hardly any combat action on the Liaodong Peninsula, which enabled the Russians to continue to improve their defensive positions around Port Arthur. Fok kept the bulk of his division on the Green Hills line, but deployed combat outposts on high ground overlooking Dalny. On 26 June, Nogi took his first offensive action by sending the 11th Infantry Division to capture Waitoushan and Prominent Peak (Kenshan), each defended by small Russian detachments. The Japanese 43rd Infantry Regiment succeeded in capturing both peaks, at the cost of 150 casualties, although the Russians conducted a serious counter-attack to try to retake them on 3 July. While Nogi had easily disposed of Fok's combat outposts, he was not confident about tackling the main line of resistance in the Green Hills until he had his entire army available. Once the port of Dalny was opened on 15 July, transports were able to bring in the 9th Infantry Division and another Kobi brigade. Despite the urgency of reopening Dalny and escorting convoys into the port, Admiral Togo put little effort into these tasks and instead focused his attention on Vitgeft's fleet.

Although Admiral Vitgeft was unwilling to interfere with the Japanese naval traffic into Dalny, Vice Admiral Pyotr A. Bezobrazov, commander of the independent cruiser squadron in Vladivostok, had no such qualms. Bezobrazov's cruiser squadron had already conducted several successful commerce raids against Japanese shipping, but Togo paid them little attention. On 15 June, Bezobrazov intercepted a Japanese troop convoy in the Tsushima strait that was en route to Dalny and sank the *Hitachi Maru* and the *Sadu Maru*. In addition to the loss of over 1,300 troops, 18 28cm siege howitzers and their crews went down with the ships. Nogi had requested

Lieutenant-General Oshima Hisanao (middle row, centre), commander of the IJA 9th Infantry Division, and his staff in October 1904. The 56-year-old Oshima had a good mix of combat command and staff experience, but none of it was geared towards positional warfare. (Author's collection)

The Japanese captured a battery of 106mm siege guns M1877 (a.k.a. the '42 Line gun') after the Russian retreat from Nanshan. These guns were used by the Third Army during the siege of Port Arthur against their former owners. (Author's collection)

these weapons be transported to Dalny in order to assist with the attack on Port Arthur, but Bezobrazov's cruisers deftly removed them from the equation. The destruction of the *Hitachi Maru* was a lucky break for the hard-pressed Russian garrison at Port Arthur and demonstrates the poor cooperation between the IJN and the IJA.

Togo was also unaware that the Russians in Port Arthur had managed to repair all their damaged battleships by mid-June. Although Vitgeft was content to remain behind his mines and coastal batteries, a consensus emerged among his junior officers that the fleet should make a break-out attempt to reach Vladivostok. The Pacific Squadron had yet to strike a real blow against the enemy, and with Port Arthur facing imminent ground attack this might be the last opportunity to escape. On 23 June, he bowed to pressure and the fleet sortied at 1630hrs with six battleships, five cruisers and seven destroyers. Vitgeft was hoping to use the approaching cover of darkness to conceal his sortie but he encountered Togo's fleet at 1800hrs. Togo, who had four battleships, six cruisers and 30 destroyers, was shocked to find that he was outnumbered in capital ships. Neither fleet was eager to engage, particularly with darkness approaching, and after an hour of steaming parallel courses Vitgeft lost his nerve and ordered his warships back to Port Arthur.

Meanwhile, Fok was trying to hold a 23km-wide front across the southern end of the Liaodong Peninsula with a reinforced division. The rugged terrain favoured the defence and the steep hills of Yupilatzu and Laotsushan anchored both ends of the line. Once he had all three divisions moved up, Nogi planned on a broad-front advance with the 1st Infantry Division in the north, and the 9th Infantry Division and the 11th Infantry Division in the centre. This plan was tactically imprudent because it failed to mass combat power at any particular point and relied upon simplistic frontal assaults. Due to the loss of his siege howitzers, he would have to rely primarily upon 75mm field guns for artillery support, which were not very effective against entrenched hilltop positions. On 26 July, Nogi began his offensive against the Green Hills line, under cover of early morning fog. The Japanese artillery was unable to suppress the Russian defences, and thus, the Japanese infantry was repulsed all along the line. The Japanese attacked again on 27 July, but still failed to make any progress. A detachment of Russian warships sortied from Port Arthur to provide naval gunfire support, but the armoured cruiser *Bayan* was badly damaged by a mine. On the night of 27/28 July, the Japanese 11th Infantry Division managed to infiltrate past the Russian position at Laotsushan, which unhinged the south end of the Russian line. Instead of counter-attacking, Fok ordered a 10km withdrawal

A pair of Russian 87mm (M1877) field guns, abandoned in the precipitate retreat back to Port Arthur. Note the hasty nature of the firing position, lacking sandbags or other cover. (Author's collection)

back to Port Arthur's outer defences on the morning of 28 July. Nogi's forces had suffered over 4,000 casualties in two days of fighting compared to about 1,000 Russian casualties, but it was Fok who blinked first. Another precipitate Russian retreat ensued, along with the loss of further valuable weapons and equipment.

Fok's new line was anchored on Wolf Hill (Feng-huang-shan) and Big Orphan Hill (Takushan), which were too far apart to be mutually supporting. Neither of the two hills had been fortified yet and the Russian troops on Wolf Hill did not have time to clear fields of fire in front of their positions, which were obscured by fields of millet. Even worse, Fok tried to impose his own inept tactical schemes on the defence, by requiring his troops to defend at the base of the hills instead of on top of the high ground. Nogi also played a joker from the deck by aggressively pursuing the Russians back to their new defensive line and not pausing to prepare another deliberate attack. Polkovnik Ivan I. Machabeli's 13th East Siberian Rifle Regiment, deployed on Wolf Hill, was caught by surprise when Japanese infantry from the 9th Infantry Division began infiltrating through the millet fields on the morning of 31 July and quickly reached the Russian trenches. Two Russian companies were overrun with the loss of over 200 troops, and the Japanese were atop Wolf Hill by noon. Even though the Russian right flank on Takushan Hill was still steady, Fok ordered his left flank to fall back to the hills around the village of Shuishiying. By the first week of August, Stoessel's troops had been pushed back to the inner defences of Port Arthur and Nogi was preparing a major attack against the fortress.

Japanese infantry waiting to advance across an open field of millet. Note that, unlike the Russians, the Japanese infantry do not have fixed bayonets. (Author's collection)

The Japanese Third Army attacks, 6–23 August 1904

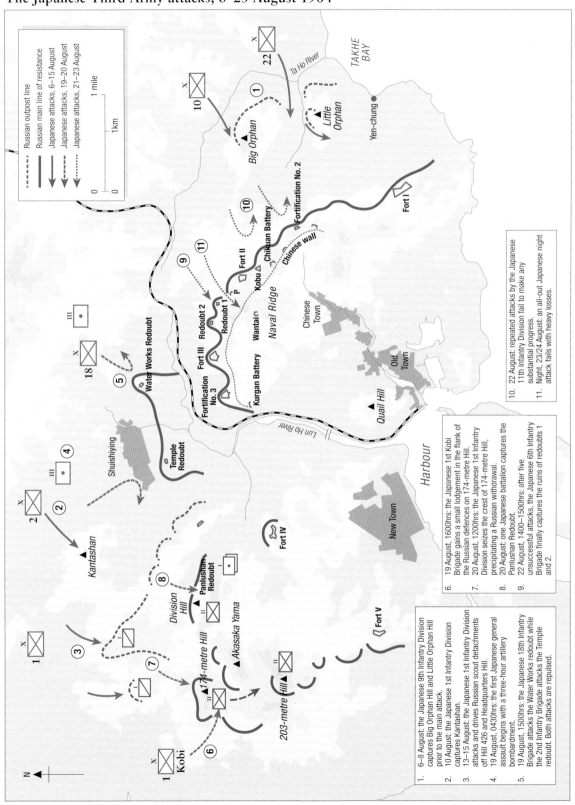

Legend:
- Russian outpost line
- Russian main line of resistance
- Japanese attacks, 6–15 August
- Japanese attacks, 19–20 August
- Japanese attacks, 21–23 August

1 mile

1km

1. 6–8 August: the Japanese 9th Infantry Division captures Big Orphan Hill and Little Orphan Hill prior to the main attack.
2. 10 August: the Japanese 1st Infantry Division captures Kantashan.
3. 13–15 August: the Japanese 1st Infantry Division attacks and drives Russian scout detachments off Hill 426 and Headquarters Hill.
4. 19 August, 0430hrs: the first Japanese general assault begins with a three-hour artillery bombardment.
5. 19 August, 1500hrs: the Japanese 18th Infantry Brigade attacks the Water Works redoubt while the 2nd Infantry Brigade attacks the Temple redoubt. Both attacks are repulsed.

6. 19 August, 1600hrs: the Japanese 1st Kobi Brigade gains a small lodgement in the flank of the Russian defences on 174-metre Hill.
7. 20 August, 1200hrs: the Japanese 1st Infantry Division seizes the crest of 174-metre Hill, precipitating a Russian withdrawal.
8. 20 August: one Japanese battalion captures the Panlushan Redoubt.
9. 22 August, 1400–1500hrs: after five unsuccessful attacks, the Japanese 6th Infantry Brigade finally captures the ruins of redoubts 1 and 2.

10. 22 August: repeated attacks by the Japanese 11th Infantry Division fail to make any substantial progress.
11. Night, 23/24 August: an all-out Japanese night attack fails with heavy losses.

Map labels:
TAKHE BAY, Ta Ho River, Little Orphan, Big Orphan, Yen-chung, Fort I, Fortification No. 2, Chikuan Battery, Chinese wall, Fort II, Kobu, Wantaic, Naval Ridge, P, Redoubt 1, Redoubt 2, Fort III, Water Works Redoubt, Fortification No. 3, Kurgan Battery, Chinese Town, Old Town, Quail Hill, Shuishiying, Temple Redoubt, Lun Ho River, Harbour, Kantashan, New Town, Fort IV, Panlushan Redoubt, Division Hill, 174-metre Hill, Akasaka Yama, Fort V, 203-metre Hill, Kobi

N

THE SIEGE BEGINS

Given his demonstrated ability to force the Russians out of well-prepared positions on the Green Hills, Nogi was confident that an all-out offensive would overcome the more hastily prepared defences outside Port Arthur. He would spend the first week of August bringing up his artillery and organizing his forces for a multi-division attack. Due to the loss of the 28cm howitzers at sea, Nogi's artillery park was less powerful than anticipated. Major-General Osako Naomichi's 2nd Field Artillery Brigade had an assortment of field guns and mortars, including some Russian 106mm guns captured at Nanshan, but no heavy artillery. The IJN thoughtfully provided enough weapons and crews to form a naval artillery group, equipped with six 12cm (4.7in.) QF guns and 20 12-pounder (7.6cm) guns. Nogi's basic concept was simple: the 1st and 9th Infantry divisions would mount a massed attack against the centre of the main Russian defensive line, which was anchored upon a series of forts and redoubts built on the Wantai Heights ('the Watcher's Terrace'). Supporting attacks on the flanks were expected to deceive the Russians as to the location of the Japanese main effort. Once the Russian line was ruptured, Nogi would commit his reserves to push on into the Old Town. However, before he could mount his main attack, Nogi had to clear up the Russian covering forces on either flank. Lieutenant-General Tsuchiya Mitsuharu's 11th Infantry Division would attack first, to capture the Russian positions on Big Orphan Hill and Little Orphan Hill (Hsia-ku-Shan), thereby unhinging the enemy right flank. After that, Lieutenant-General Tsumumoto Matsumura's 1st Infantry Division would eliminate the Russian covering force detachments deployed north-east of 174-metre Hill.

The biggest problem facing the defenders was a muddled leadership structure, which violated every precept of unity of command. The front was divided into two sectors: Sector I (under the command of General-mayor Vladimir N. Gorbatovsky) was responsible for the eastern and northern fronts, while Sector II (under General-mayor Vladimir A. Irmanov) was responsible for the western front. A large covering force, consisting of 26 companies, was deployed forward of the main positions and spread across both sectors. General Kondratenko was in charge of the land defence, but reported to Stoessel and Smirnov. Fok was put in charge of the reserve, which consisted of 16 infantry companies and two artillery batteries. Rather than keeping unit integrity, the sub-units of both the 4th and 7th East Siberian Rifle divisions were intermixed and spread across all three fronts, further diluting the existing command structures. Although the East Siberian Rifle regiments in the garrison had taken significant casualties since May, they were still at about 80–85 per cent of authorized strength

One of the early Japanese infantry assaults on a Russian-held hilltop, apparently under Russian artillery fire. The siege of Port Arthur demonstrated that exposed assault troops could not survive for long in daylight under these conditions, and the Japanese quickly shifted to night attacks. (Author's collection)

and they had been reinforced with seven companies of sailors and several volunteer detachments.

Nogi paid little attention to the enemy, terrain or weather in planning his attack. Indeed, Nogi did not know how to read a military map, and his staff was also noticeably incompetent. In his guidance, he stated that, 'all attacks which are time-consuming should be avoided. There is no time to consider whether or not the fortifications are strong or weak.' Big Orphan Hill and its neighbour Little Orphan Hill were located behind the Ta Ho River, which was a water obstacle that was about 30–40m wide and of uncertain depth. The weather was very rainy in early August, which made any effort to cross the Ta Ho under fire even more problematic. Both hills were also extremely steep and difficult to climb. The Russians had three battalions defending the area around both hills, and they had succeeded in emplacing four field guns and some machine guns atop Big Orphan. It was a strong position. At 0430hrs on 7 August, Naomichi's artillery began a three-hour artillery preparation on Big Orphan Hill, using three batteries of 12cm naval guns, four batteries of 9cm mortars and the divisional artillery equipped with 7.5cm field guns. The Japanese bombardment did inflict modest damage on the defenders atop Big Orphan Hill, forcing them to seek cover on the reverse slopes, but rainy weather obscured the target. Tsuchiya's 11th Infantry Division then advanced to the Ta Ho, with the 10th Infantry Brigade on the right and the 22nd Infantry Brigade on the left. The Japanese infantry became disorganized in crossing the Ta Ho and suffered heavy casualties from Russian fire, so only a single battalion made it to the southern slope of Big Orphan Hill by nightfall at 2030hrs. Under these conditions, Tsuchiya opted to pause his attack in order to reorganize during the night.

Yet the rainy weather did not relent the next morning on 8 August, so Tsuchiya decided to await more favourable conditions. Unexpectedly, a Russian naval squadron, led by the cruiser *Novik*, appeared in Takhe Bay and began to pour a galling enfilade fire into the assembly area of the Japanese 43rd Infantry Regiment, inflicting heavy casualties. Togo's patrol ships had missed the Russian sortie in the poor visibility, and consequently, no

A Russian gun position in Fort II, early in the siege. The structure of the five largest Russian forts was composed of reinforced concrete and brick masonry, which was intended to withstand hits from up to 15cm shells. (Author's collection)

Japanese warships were in the immediate vicinity. Eventually, two Japanese armoured cruisers were summoned, but the *Novik* and her consorts escaped unscathed. The incident led to considerable rancour between the Japanese army and navy leadership. Tsuchiya's disorganized 11th Infantry Division was unable to resume the attack until late afternoon, and his infantry did not advance until 1900hrs. Nevertheless, this time the Japanese infantry made better headway because the Russian troops on the hilltop were low on ammunition and apparently were caught off-guard. By 2030hrs, the soldiers of the 22nd Infantry Brigade reached the summit and the Russian defenders withdrew. Little Orphan was taken by an assault at dawn the next morning. The loss of the two hills was a serious blow to the Russian defences on the eastern front of Port Arthur, but Nogi made no further efforts along this axis of advance. Altogether, these supporting attacks cost the 11th Infantry Division 1,280 dead and wounded, compared with 450 Russian casualties.

A naval brigade played a prominent role in the initial Japanese attacks on Port Arthur. The brigade was equipped with six 12cm (4.7in.) QF guns and 20 12-pounder (7.6cm guns), mostly taken from older Japanese warships. Two of the 12cm guns were set up on a prominent height where they could partially observe Port Arthur, from a distance of about 8–9km. On the morning of 7 August, these two guns had begun an intermittent bombardment of the port, firing at extreme range. By sheer luck, they managed to hit the battleship *Tsesarevich* twice and to wound Admiral Vitgeft in the leg. A renewed bombardment on 9 August scored seven hits on the battleship *Retvizan*. A message soon arrived from the Tsar, ordering Vitgeft to immediately take the fleet to Vladivostok before it was lost to bombardment. On the morning of 10 August, Vitgeft sortied from Port Arthur with six battleships, four cruisers and ten destroyers. Togo was caught off-balance because he had divided his fleet, sending a cruiser–destroyer force to prevent a repetition of the Russian naval bombardment of the 11th Infantry Division. He was left with only four battleships and two armoured cruisers to block Vitgeft's break-out attempt. Nevertheless, Togo moved to intercept, which resulted in the Battle of the Yellow Sea.[18] In summary, the Russian fleet nearly escaped after a lengthy gunnery action which inflicted great punishment on both sides, but Vitgeft was killed at a critical moment and the Russian fleet thrown into disorder. Five Russian battleships, one cruiser and ten destroyers eventually staggered back to Port Arthur. The battleship *Tsesarevich*, two cruisers and four destroyers managed to reach neutral ports, where they were interned. Although Togo had not sunk any Russian warships, the remaining vessels had been battered into irrelevance because they no longer had much remaining combat capability. After the Battle of the Yellow Sea, more guns and more sailors were taken from the immobilized warships to reinforce the land defence of Port Arthur.

On 10 August, Matsumura's 1st Infantry Division began its own preliminary attacks by driving a Russian scout detachment off Kantashan, located about 4km north-east of 174-metre Hill. In Sector II, the Russians had an outer line of combat outposts atop Headquarters Hill and Hill 426, held by three scout detachments with a total of about 300 troops. Tretyakov's 5th East Siberian Rifle Regiment held the main line of resistance, anchored upon 174-metre Hill, 203-metre Hill (known to the Russians as Vysokaya) and

18 This battle has been covered in detail in my earlier work *Russian Battleship vs Japanese Battleship: Yellow Sea 1904–05* (Osprey Duel series no. 15, 2009).

A destroyed Russian Hotchkiss 47mm gun atop 174-metre Hill. The Japanese artillery slowly smashed Russian fieldworks to bits and disabled their crew-served weapons. (Author's collection)

Division Hill (Panlushan), with eight rifle companies, and two artillery batteries. Although the Russians had dug some trenches and emplaced some barbed wire, none of these positions were particularly strong. On the night of 13/14 August, the Japanese 1st Infantry Brigade advanced with several battalions against the Russian outer line of combat outposts. Even though the Japanese had a huge numerical advantage – in the order of 8:1 – the initial attacks fumbled when they ran into barbed-wire obstacles in the dark. The Russian defenders fired off flares which illuminated the attackers and threw them into further disorder. The Japanese mounted several banzai attacks before dawn on 14 August, but these failed as well. Stymied, the Japanese resorted to artillery bombardment to drive the defenders from the hilltops. The Japanese artillery fired Shimosa-filled high-explosive shells, which inflicted heavy losses upon the Russian infantry, who lacked deep trenches or bunkers. Kondratenko sent Tretyakov two companies of sailors and two companies of infantry from the 4th Reserve Battalion to reinforce the outpost line, but this only delayed the inevitable. By the end of 14 August, Tretyakov's outpost line had been badly battered. On the morning of 15 August, the Russians attempted a relief in place atop Headquarters Hill but Japanese artillery pounded the position just as the reservists arrived and they bolted to the rear. Soon, all the remaining Russian troops abandoned Hill 426 and Headquarters Hill, despite Tretyakov's efforts to rally them. The Japanese lost over 400 troops just taking Hill 426 and the Russians about 250 troops overall, but the covering-force battle had been lost.

With the Russian flank defences eliminated, Nogi sent a staff officer into Port Arthur under a white flag on the morning of 16 August, in order to offer surrender terms. In the note, Nogi alluded to a possible repetition of the Port Arthur massacre of 1894, warning of the 'useless loss of life and any possible violence, murder or looting by Japanese troops fighting their way into the town, which it would be difficult to prevent'. Stoessel and Smirnov drafted a joint reply, which curtly rejected the Japanese surrender offer. Nogi had also offered to allow civilians to leave the city. By the start of the siege, two-thirds of the pre-war population had already left the city, but about 2,000 Russian and 14,000 Chinese civilians remained in Port Arthur, along with about 40,000 soldiers and sailors.

At approximately 0430hrs on 19 August, one hour before dawn, the Japanese Third Army began its artillery preparation against the Russian front-line positions, with the heaviest bombardment on Fort No. III and the Water Works Redoubt in the centre. In Sector II, Major-General Tomoyasu Harunobu's 1st Kobi (Reserve) Infantry Brigade began advancing at 0600hrs

Russian sailors are organized into companies before being sent to the front as naval infantry. The sailors were enthusiastic in the counter-attack role but proved unreliable in static defence due to a lack of field training and a tendency to wander off in search of food. (Author's collection)

towards the west side of 174-metre Hill, while the rest of Matsumura's 1st Infantry Division waited. Since the loss of his outpost line, Tretyakov and his men had been working hard to improve the defences of this position, digging more trenches and laying more barbed wire. Podpolkovnik Nikolai A. Lisaevsky was in command atop 174-metre Hill and Tretyakov was nearby on Akasaka Yama, with Irmanov, the sector commander. In addition to six infantry companies spread across about 2km of frontage (two on 174-metre Hill itself and four on the connecting ridge), Lisaevsky had four Hotchkiss QF field guns and two machine guns, plus four field mortars. General-mayor Vasily F. Bely, the fortress artillery commander, had also prevailed upon Tretyakov to install two naval 6in. Canet guns atop the hill, but these two large weapons had poor fields of fire. Initially, the Japanese infantry made little progress, due to obstacles and defensive fire. Consequently, Matsumura resorted to firepower, and ordered his artillery to rain Shimosa-filled shells onto the top of 174-metre Hill, which inflicted 50 per cent losses on the two Russian infantry companies near the crest. By late afternoon, the Japanese had also noticed that many of the Russian artillery batteries were poorly sited and could not cover significant amounts of dead space on the western slope of the hill. Around 1600hrs, a great mass of infantry from the 1st Kobi Brigade advanced through this dead space; Russian artillery fire drove most of them back, but about 100 men were able to reach the first Russian trench line in the saddle behind 174-metre Hill. The Japanese managed to occupy a very annoying position, which the Russians could not easily access from their own trenches without crossing exposed ground. Nevertheless, Lisaevsky tried to organize a counter-attack, but Japanese artillery fire inflicted heavy casualties and broke up the attempt. For his trouble, Lisaevsky was hit in the face by shrapnel, leaving Shtabs-kapitan Aleksandr A. Belozerov in command. Just before sunset, General Kondratenko arrived with four companies of the 13th East Siberian Rifle Regiment and urged Tretyakov to mount a night counter-attack. However, due to a variety of miscues, the night counter-attack fizzled out and Tretyakov contented himself with repairing his positions. The Japanese Shimosa shells had demolished a good portion of the defensive works atop 174-metre Hill and most of the Russian field guns had been knocked out.

At dawn on 20 August, the Japanese bombardment of 174-metre Hill resumed and the 1st Kobi Brigade tried to get reinforcements through to its pinned troops but failed. Nor could the Russians eliminate the enemy lodgment in their flank, despite several desperate counter-attacks. By 1100hrs, the Russian trenches had been demolished and Kapitan Belozerov was mortally wounded. Command of the survivors atop 174-metre Hill fell to Podporuchik Fedor N. Ivanov. Sensing that the Russian defence on the hill was wavering, Matsumura committed Major-General Yamamoto Nobuyuki's 1st Infantry Brigade to attack from the north-east. Down to fewer than 100 troops, Ivanov immediately requested reinforcements. Kondratenko and Tretyakov agreed to release their single reserve infantry company, but Fok appeared and rejected the plan to reinforce 174-metre Hill. For reasons that remain unclear, Kondratenko and Tretyakov – both brave and competent front-line officers – acquiesced to this foolish decision. Consequently, about half of Ivanov's troops retreated down the hill and the other 50 fought to the death. By early afternoon, the Japanese infantry had captured 174-metre Hill, forcing Tretyakov to pull back his troops from the now untenable connecting ridge. In addition, the Japanese 1st Infantry Division launched a successful attack, taking advantage of dead space in ravines, to overrun the Russian artillery batteries at the Panlushan Redoubt. According to Tretyakov's memoirs, the Russians suffered 1,000 casualties (one-third of which had been killed) in the defence of 174-metre Hill and surrounding positions. Other sources claim that the Japanese suffered about 1,700 casualties in this sector.

Meanwhile, Lieutenant-General Oshima's 9th Infantry Division was tasked with capturing the Water Works (Vodoprovodny) Redoubt and the Temple (Kumirnensky) Redoubt, on the hills just south of the village of Shuishiying. The two redoubts were held by four infantry companies (11./26th East Siberian Rifle Regiment; and 9., 10. and 11./15th East Siberian Rifle Regiment) under the command of Polkovnik Vladimir G. Semenov (commander of the 26th East Siberian Rifle Regiment). The redoubts were entrenched and had two 63mm field guns and three machine guns for close-in defence, and were supported by an entrenched battery with four 77mm guns and four 9in. mortars. On the morning of 19 August, Oshima ordered his artillery to batter both redoubts for hours, which inflicted heavy damage on the Russian trenches. Then, at 1500hrs, Oshima sent his 18th Infantry Brigade to attack the Water Works Redoubt, while the 2nd Brigade from Matsumura's 1st Infantry Division attacked the Temple Redoubt. Despite the damage, the Russian artillery and machine guns were still intact and their fire inflicted 80 per

A Russian 9in. siege mortar M1877; this weapon was used to engage enemy troops in 'dead space' areas. The mortar had a very low rate of fire but it fired a high-explosive round that could inflict significant damage on enemy sappers. (Author's collection)

cent losses on the lead Japanese assault company. Both Japanese brigades were repulsed. Semenov even managed to launch a local counter-attack which threw the Japanese infantry back on their heels. Oshima made another attack on the morning of 20 August, which also failed. Japanese infantrymen were able to infiltrate into the ruins of Shuishiying and to occupy some ground on the flanks, but the Russian defence in the centre remained solid. General-mayor Bely directed the Russian artillery counter-fire during the battle and inflicted heavy losses on the Japanese infantry, although he could do little to suppress the enemy guns. In addition, five Russian battleships in the inner harbour provided naval gunfire support, when feasible.

Nogi made no real attempt against the Wantai Heights during the opening days of his first general offensive. Instead, Nogi used his artillery to methodically destroy both redoubts nos. 1 and 2, knocking out five of their guns and killing most of the crews. Both Fort II and Fort III also suffered significant damage, with most of their guns silenced, as well. However, both of these forts had concrete structures and strong parapets, which could absorb more punishment than common fieldworks. It was not until the night of 21/22 August that Nogi made a serious attempt to carry some of the battered enemy works. Major-General Ichinohe Hyoe's 6th Infantry Brigade advanced towards Redoubt No. 1 but was stopped by barbed wire at the base of the slope and then shot to pieces by Russian machine-gun and shrapnel fire. Five attempts were made by Ichinohe's troops, but each failed in turn. The next day, 22 August, Nogi reinforced the 9th Infantry Division with the 4th Kobi Infantry Brigade and ordered another assault against the ruins of redoubts nos. 1 and 2. Tsuchiya's 11th Infantry Division was ordered to make a supporting attack with its 10th Infantry Brigade against Fort II. The 10th Infantry Brigade briefly managed to gain a foothold on the heights before being pushed off by Russian counter-attacks. General Ichinohe ordered his attack to jump off at 1015hrs, using some dead space to get his assault troops within 200m of the Russian front line. The Japanese infantry from the 7th and 35th Infantry regiments sprang forward after a short artillery preparation, and this time they were able to cut their way through the enemy barbed wire. Surging forward, the Japanese infantry reached the edge of Redoubt No. 1, and after deadly close-quarter fighting, managed to secure the position by about 1400hrs. The commander of the 7th Infantry Regiment and two battalion commanders were killed in the assault, but Ichinohe, who personally led the attack, pivoted his remaining troops and captured Redoubt No. 2 by 1500hrs. The local Russian commander appealed for reinforcements to save these positions, but Fok refused to release any of the reserve companies. The capture of the two redoubts in a daylight assault was a major *coup de main* for the Japanese, but it cost Ichinohe's 6th Infantry Brigade 2,100 casualties out of its starting strength of 2,548 troops.

Major-General Ichinohe Hyoe, commander of the 6th Infantry Brigade. Ichinohe's aggressive front-line leadership enabled the Japanese Third Army to gain a toehold on the Wantai Heights which was gradually expanded. After the war, Ichinohe enjoyed a stellar career in the IJA. (Author's collection)

The Japanese siege howitzers and underground mines inflicted heavy damage on the Russian forts, but never actually destroyed them. In particular, the underground galleries remained impervious to most of the enemy bombardments. (Author's collection)

JAPANESE FORLORN HOPE, 23/24 AUGUST 1904 (PP. 60–61)

After five days of pounding on the outer defences of Port Arthur in his first general attack, Nogi's Third Army had only succeeded in capturing a few minor positions, at great cost. Hoping to achieve tactical surprise, Nogi decided to mount a night attack on the eastern side of the Russian defences, on the Wantai Heights. Seven battalions from the 6th Infantry Brigade and the 4th Kobi (Reserve) Brigade would mount an infiltration attack up a 175m-wide ravine, just east of the Russian Redoubt No. 1, in order to capture a position known as the 'Large Eagle's Nest'. If successful, another infantry brigade would reinforce the attack. However, the attack was poorly conceived, since Russian troops in the sector were fully alert and could pour down flanking fire from Redoubt No. 1. Although battered by constant artillery barrages, the Russian defences on the Wantai Heights were still intact. Nogi seemed to think that one more massed attack would break the Russian line, but regarded the attack as something of a forlorn hope. Nevertheless, at 2200hrs on 23 August, the Japanese 7th Infantry Regiment led the attack up the ravine.

In this scene, soldiers from the 7th Regiment are attempting to breach the barbed-wire obstacles with improvised wire cutters (**1**). However, the Russians have electrified and booby-trapped the wire entanglements, causing casualties among the breaching teams. Dead and wounded from previous breach attempts are still in the wire. Groups of Japanese infantry are behind them (**2**), waiting in the shadows for the breach to be made. However, the Russian defenders on the heights have quickly noticed the breach attempt and have begun firing magnesium flares (**3**) to illuminate the Japanese troops in the ravine, followed by fire from machine guns and light artillery. The Russians are also using searchlights – a first on the battlefield – to spotlight enemy troop concentrations.

Under the glare of the searchlights, flares and heavy fire, many of the Japanese troops became dazed and confused in the engagement area. The Russian troops began throwing improvised grenades and even large stones down on the Japanese troops in the ravine, which quickly became a slaughter pit. Although a few Japanese infantrymen were able to reach the heights, they could not capture them, and after five hours of fighting the ravine was littered with thousands of Japanese dead and wounded. Nogi's first general assault had failed miserably.

Nogi intended to use these two captured positions as a springboard to launch an all-out night attack to break through on the Wantai Heights, and he quickly set this plan in motion. The attack, which began around 2200hrs on 23 August, is depicted in the accompanying battlescene artwork. It was a complete fiasco that cost the 9th Infantry Division thousands of additional casualties and exhausted its supply of small-arms ammunition. Likewise, the Japanese field artillery was also desperately short of ammunition and could not support any additional attacks until resupplied. After the failure of the night attack on 23/24 August, it was evident that the first general assault had bent, but not broken, the Russian defences. Nogi's Third Army suffered 15,860 casualties (including 5,017 dead) during the offensive. In addition, his army had already suffered several thousand combat casualties in the first two weeks of August and about 10,000 Japanese troops were incapacitated by illness due to poor field hygiene. Consequently, Nogi's Third Army was reduced by nearly 30,000 troops, or about 40 per cent of its strength. The Russian garrison suffered 6,000 casualties in repulsing the Japanese offensive, including about 1,500 dead.

In Tokyo, Kodama and the rest of the General Staff were shocked by the scale of losses suffered during Nogi's first general offensive. It was agreed to immediately send 16,000 replacements to rebuild the Third Army's shattered infantry regiments. However, Nogi was urged to shift to more methodical methods, rather than simply hurling massed infantry against enemy defensive positions. One lesson learned from the failed offensive was that artillery was the key to reducing enemy trenches and redoubts, so the General Staff expedited the transfer of another detachment of six 28cm howitzers to make up for the ones lost on the *Hitachi Maru*, as well as a resupply of artillery ammunition for the 2nd Field Artillery Brigade. A ship with the first batch of 28cm howitzers reached Dalny on 31 August, but these 5-ton weapons had to be laboriously dragged over 40km to the front and reassembled, which would take weeks to make a battery operational. Japanese infantry had – for the most part – proved incredibly brave in the attack and willing to suffer enormous losses, but their tactics had been too primitive for existing battlefield conditions. Bunching up in enemy kill zones enabled even small numbers of Russian defenders to inflict crippling casualties. Tactical dispersion and infiltration through dead space or cover were the elusive keys to success.

From the Russian point of view, their front-line infantry had performed magnificently, doggedly defending positions that had been reduced to rubble

The destroyer *Besposhchadnyy* (*Merciless*) at Port Arthur in 1904. The Russian lighter warships proved more useful during the siege due to their shallow drafts and were able to provide naval gunfire support. In August, the *Besposhchadnyy* escaped to internment in Qingdao, and returned to Russian service after the war. (Author's collection)

by incessant enemy artillery fire. Russian personnel losses were much lighter but could only be replaced by sailors and volunteers. The sailors added great shock effect in local counter-attacks, but they were ill suited to trench warfare and displayed a consistent tendency to wander off from assigned positions. In material terms, the Russian garrison still had plenty of artillery and had only expended 20 per cent of its stockpile of ammunition, stopping the first general offensive. However, Russian leadership had been problematic, particularly with Fok's ability to hinder the timely commitment of reserves to threatened sectors. Smirnov tried to relieve Fok of command, but was overruled by Stoessel. Multiple overlapping chains of command led to a sclerotic decision-making process which enabled the Japanese to capitalize on fleeting battlefield opportunities. The Russian defence was also hindered by the rocky terrain, which made it difficult for troops to dig in deep enough to reduce the effect of enemy artillery bombardments. One lesson learned by the Russians from Nogi's first general offensive was to make better use of reverse-slope positions and to begin tunnelling into the rock to create deeper shell-proof redoubts. At the tactical level, the Russians had learned how to position their machine guns to create interlocking fields of fire and to use small, quick-firing guns to cover dead space. The key to a successful defence was to keep only small numbers of troops in exposed front-line positions, but to be ready to counter-attack with reserve infantry companies before the enemy could seize these positions.

THE SHIFT TO TRENCH WARFARE

The Russians made several attempts to recover the ruins of redoubts nos. 1 and 2 in late August, but these all failed. On the other hand, General Ichinohe and the remnants of his brigade were quite isolated in the two redoubts, and remained so until communication trenches could be dug to allow covered movement up the slope. On 1 September, Japanese engineers began constructing saps and parallels on several parts of the front, in order to allow troops and guns to move closer to enemy lines under cover. Nogi intended to conduct another major offensive as soon as the replacements and ammunition arrived, but he was unwilling to wait for the 28cm howitzers. He wanted to feint on his left, against the Wantai Heights, but make the main effort in the centre to capture the Water Works and Temple redoubts. A supporting attack would be made on his right flank, against Namako Yama and 203-metre Hill. Only the 1st and 9th Infantry divisions and the 1st Kobi Brigade would be used in this offensive, with the 11th Infantry Division simply employed as a flank guard.

Nogi's plan remained very unimaginative and was essentially just a more focused frontal attack. Some staff officers raised the idea of going after the more thinly held Russian flanks, but Nogi was not interested. An attack by the 11th Infantry Division

Japanese engineers working on extending a communications trench. Given that it is daylight and the troops are standing upright, this position is probably well out of range of the Russian defences. (Author's collection)

A test fire of the Russian 'land torpedo', developed by naval engineers in Port Arthur. Essentially, this was an improvised mortar that fired a long torpedo-like projectile out to about 100m. Packed full of explosives, the 'torpedo' could inflict significant damage on Japanese sappers as they approached Russian trenches. (Author's collection)

against the Russian right flank, between Fort I and the coast, could have been supported by naval gunfire from Togo's battleships – but neither the army nor navy leaders were in favour of a joint operation of that sort. Even a flanking attack by one of the Kobi brigades against the extended Russian left flank could have drawn scarce reserves away from the main battle area. However, Nogi was not inclined to fancy manoeuvreing or working with the navy to increase his combat power, so he opted for the simplest solution. By early September, Japanese engineers had built parallels within 35–70m of the Water Works and Temple redoubts, leaving little doubt as to Nogi's intentions. At such close proximity, both sides suffered daily casualties from sniping and mortar fire, which quickly exhausted the troops. The Russians learned to keep only one platoon from each company in the trenches at a time, while rotating the remainder to reserve positions where they could eat and sleep.

Even an incompetent officer such as Stoessel could see what was coming, and he ordered Kondratenko to strengthen the defences in both redoubts as well as to build a new line of trenches to prevent the Japanese from expanding their gains around redoubts nos. 1 and 2. However, Stoessel forbade his troops from conducting sorties to disrupt the Japanese sapping activity (some unauthorized sorties did occur), which he claimed was too costly in manpower losses. The Russians used the three weeks between Japanese offensives to lay over 600 mines and fougasses around key forward positions. Another 32 light guns (mostly 37mm and 47mm QF guns) were dismounted from the fleet and distributed among forward positions, as well. The Russians set up an armaments factory in one of the warehouses in Port Arthur, manufacturing hand grenades and other improvised explosives. An experimental 225mm mine-thrower was developed, which could hurl a torpedo-shaped mine out to about 100m – it would come as a nasty surprise to Japanese troops. The only point of contention was 203-metre Hill, which Stoessel did not regard as a particularly important position. Nevertheless, Tretyakov and Kondratenko ordered more trenches built to protect 203-metre Hill, and ensured that it had a strong garrison. A small road was built to the top of 203-metre Hill, enabling reinforcements to reach the crest more quickly.

On the morning of 19 September, Nogi began his second general assault at 0630hrs with a staggered artillery preparation. Initially, the Imperial Japanese Naval Brigade (20 guns) pounded Russian positions on the Wantai Heights in order to suggest that the 6th Infantry Brigade might attempt to break out from its small perimeter around the ruins of redoubts nos. 1 and 2. Then, at 1200hrs, the 2nd Field Artillery Brigade (88 guns) opened fire against the two main redoubts in the northern sector. Over 1,000 rounds were fired at the Water Works Redoubt, reducing it to rubble. The Temple Redoubt was also hard hit. It was not until 1800hrs that Major-General Nakamura Satoru's 2nd Infantry Brigade began its assault against the north-east corner of the Water Works Redoubt. Although the defenders were stunned by the bombardment, they put up stiff resistance and Russian artillery support from Fort III used enfilade fire to inflict heavy casualties. The Japanese infantry staggered to the first line of trenches and sought cover, which gave the Russians a brief respite. Kondratenko was able to quickly send forward two reserve companies, which spearheaded a counter-attack that pushed the Japanese back from the trenches at the point of the bayonet. Nevertheless, with dusk falling, Nakamura ordered another attack, and close-quarter fighting continued most of the night around the Water Works Redoubt. Flares lit up the night, illuminating stacks of bodies in shattered trenches. The Russians dropped hand grenades into the first row of trenches below the redoubt, but they were only holding on by their fingernails. At 0500hrs on 20 September, the Japanese 9th Infantry Division committed two infantry regiments from Major-General Hirasara Ryozo's 18th Infantry Brigade against the eastern side of the Water Works Redoubt, causing the last 11 Russian survivors to evacuate the position with one remaining machine gun. Once the Water Works Redoubt was occupied, the Temple Redoubt became untenable and the two Russian companies still there withdrew.

The Japanese 1st Infantry Division committed Major-General Yamamoto Nobuyuki's 1st Infantry Brigade against Namako Yama, just to the south-east of 174-metre Hill. Tretyakov had two infantry companies defending the hill, along with a detachment of sailors and some artillery crews. During the night of 18/19 September, the Japanese conducted a surprise attack with one company, which caught the defenders off-guard and succeeded in capturing part of the lower trenches on the north-east corner without firing a shot. Chagrined by this easy loss, Tretyakov ordered a counter-attack to drive out the intruders, but it did not occur. On the morning of 19 September, the Japanese artillery began bombarding the top of Namako Yama, including four 47mm Hotchkiss QF guns that had been stealthily brought close onto 174-metre Hill. The point-blank fire inflicted 75 casualties on the 9./5th East Siberian Rifle Regiment, including all its officers. Tretyakov sent a reserve company to reinforce the defence, but as dusk approached, four Japanese battalions left their trenches and began advancing towards the hill. Despite the long odds, the Russian infantry and gunners managed to hold onto Namako Yama for several more hours and General Yamamoto was mortally wounded in the attack. Nevertheless, the last Russian survivors finally evacuated the position on the night of 19/20 September.

Apparently Stoessel was not the only one who failed to appreciate the importance of 203-metre Hill, since Nogi only assigned the reservists of the 1st Kobi Brigade to capture this key position. Tretyakov had strengthened 203-metre Hill with a garrison of three infantry companies and one naval

The Japanese had a large number of obsolescent siege weapons at Port Arthur, including 72 of these 15cm mortars. During the course of the siege. The 15cm mortars fired over 30,000 rounds at the Russian positions. (Author's collection)

company, supported by six guns (including two naval 6in. guns) and four machine guns. At least one 225mm mine-thrower was also stationed on the hill. In addition, Russian battleships in the inner harbour were able to provide naval gunfire support, when requested. At 2030hrs, Major-General Tomoyasu Harunobu's 1st Kobi Brigade advanced against the west side of 203-metre Hill. However, the Russian garrison, under Podpolkovnik Stanislav Y. Stempnevsky, was alert and inflicted heavy losses on the attackers. Nevertheless, the Japanese breached the Russian wire in two places and were able to occupy the lower trenches. Stempnevsky appealed to Kondratenko for reinforcements, who responded by quickly sending three reserve companies, which led a successful counter-attack. The fresh Russian troops drove the Japanese back from the wire, ending the threat for the moment. Nogi ordered the 1st Kobi Brigade to launch another major attack on 203-metre Hill on the night of 20/21 September, which reoccupied the lower trenches. Kondratenko fed more reinforcements into the battle, and the Russian infantrymen rolled improvised grenades down into the Japanese-held trench. However, the four Russian infantry companies on 203-metre Hill had been gutted, suffering over 300 casualties, with no local reserves remaining.

Nogi ordered the exhausted reserve brigade to keep attacking, reinforced by troops from the 1st Infantry Division. The Japanese kept up the pressure on 203-metre Hill all day on 21 September, blasting the crest with heavy artillery while their infantry probed for weak spots in the defences. On the evening of 21 September, Tretyakov conducted a skilful relief-in-place operation, replacing three depleted companies on 203-metre Hill with three fresh companies loaned from Kondratenko's sector reserves. For the third major assault on 203-metre Hill, three Japanese battalions assembled in dead space north-west of the hill on the morning of 22 September. However, this time the Russians got a lucky break when one of their forward observers spotted the enemy troop concentration and reported the information to Kondratenko. He immediately ordered a section of two guns to move forward to a concealed position in a field of millet, from which they had a clear line of fire into the flank of the enemy assembly area. In just over five minutes, the Russian gunners fired 51 rounds of shrapnel into the three Japanese battalions, inflicting severe losses and causing the survivors to flee in panic.

NOGI'S SECOND GENERAL ASSAULT, 19–22 SEPTEMBER 1904

For his second attempt, Nogi decided to focus his main effort against the Water Works and Temple redoubts. A secondary effort against 203-metre Hill and Namako Yama was expected to disrupt the Russian western flank. This was the first modern trench battle, with both sides making extensive use of fieldworks and involving considerable close-quarter fighting.

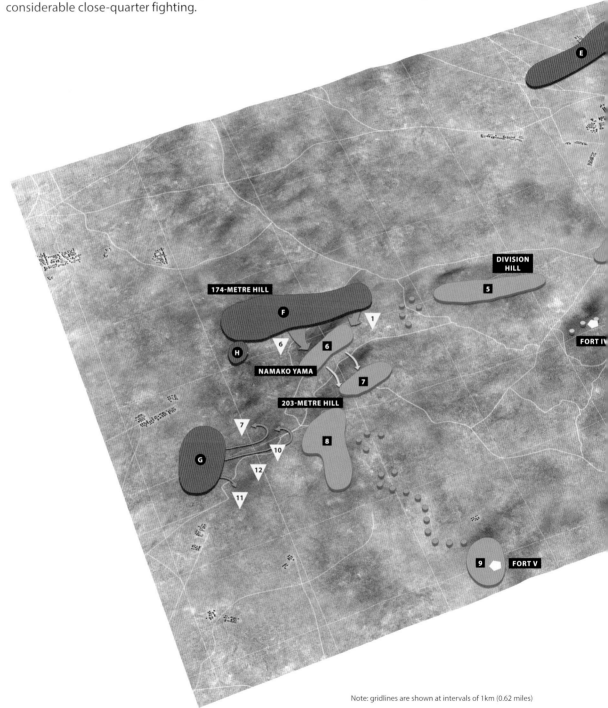

Note: gridlines are shown at intervals of 1km (0.62 miles)

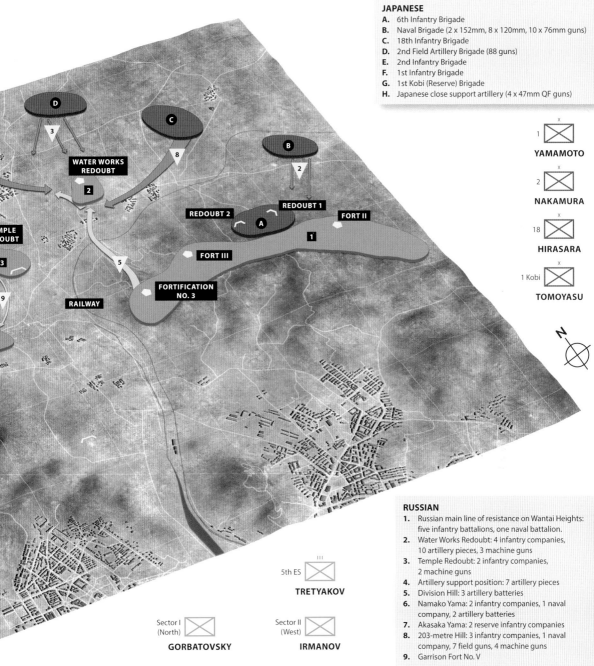

JAPANESE

A. 6th Infantry Brigade
B. Naval Brigade (2 x 152mm, 8 x 120mm, 10 x 76mm guns)
C. 18th Infantry Brigade
D. 2nd Field Artillery Brigade (88 guns)
E. 2nd Infantry Brigade
F. 1st Infantry Brigade
G. 1st Kobi (Reserve) Brigade
H. Japanese close support artillery (4 x 47mm QF guns)

1 | YAMAMOTO

2 | NAKAMURA

18 | HIRASARA

1 Kobi | TOMOYASU

RUSSIAN

1. Russian main line of resistance on Wantai Heights: five infantry battalions, one naval battalion.
2. Water Works Redoubt: 4 infantry companies, 10 artillery pieces, 3 machine guns
3. Temple Redoubt: 2 infantry companies, 2 machine guns
4. Artillery support position: 7 artillery pieces
5. Division Hill: 3 artillery batteries
6. Namako Yama: 2 infantry companies, 1 naval company, 2 artillery batteries
7. Akasaka Yama: 2 reserve infantry companies
8. 203-metre Hill: 3 infantry companies, 1 naval company, 7 field guns, 4 machine guns
9. Garrison Fort No. V

5th ES | TRETYAKOV

Sector I (North) | GORBATOVSKY

Sector II (West) | IRMANOV

EVENTS

1. Night, 18/19 September: the Japanese 1st Infantry Brigade captures a small foothold on Namako Yama with a surprise night attack.

2. 0630hrs, 19 September: the Japanese Naval Brigade bombards Russian positions on the Wantai Heights as an attempt to distract from where the main attack will occur.

3. 1200hrs, 19 September: the Japanese 2nd Field Artillery Brigade begins a six-hour bombardment of the Water Works and Temple redoubts, inflicting great damage.

4. 1800hrs, 19 September: the Japanese 2nd Infantry Brigade attacks the Water Works Redoubt, but suffers heavy losses.

5. 1900hrs, 19 September: Kondratenko sends two reserve companies, which lead a successful counter-attack at the Water Works Redoubt.

6. 1900hrs, 19 September: the Japanese 1st Infantry Brigade advances to Namako Yama with four battalions. Heavy fighting continues throughout the night.

7. 2200hrs, 19 September: the Japanese 1st Kobi Brigade attacks 203-metre Hill, but is repulsed.

8. 0500hrs, 20 September: the Japanese 18th Infantry Brigade attacks the neck of the Water Works Redoubt, threatening to cut it off. The Russian survivors evacuate.

9. 0600hrs, 20 September: the Russian garrison evacuates the Temple Redoubt.

10. 1400hrs, 20 September: the last Russian survivors evacuate Namako Yama.

11. Night 20/21 September: the 1st Kobi Brigade launches another attack on 203-metre Hill, which nearly succeeds.

12. Morning, 22 September: Russian field guns disrupt the third attempt by the 1st Kobi Brigade to assault 203-metre Hill, rendering the unit combat ineffective.

The 28cm howitzer fired two types of projectiles: an iron shell filled with 9.5kg of black powder and a steel shell filled with 80kg of Shimosa. Note that the weapon is emplaced in a reverse-slope position, but in an open revetment with no protection for the crews. (Author's collection)

Russian front-line troops had to endure constant bombardment and night attacks, while their positions were reduced to cratered ruins. Nevertheless, the morale of the Russian soldiers remained solid right up to the end of the siege. (Author's collection)

In addition, the Russians organized a counter-attack on 203-metre Hill using the fresh infantry and a resupply of hand grenades to evict the Japanese from the lower trenches. After this disaster, the 1st Kobi Brigade was no longer combat effective and Nogi lacked sufficient infantry reserves to continue attacking 203-metre Hill. Nor did the Japanese artillery have enough ammunition remaining to support another large-scale attack. Consequently, after four days of fighting Nogi was compelled to suspend his second general offensive.

Overall, Nogi's second general offensive achieved most of its immediate tactical objectives, but failed to break the Russian defence, thus failing in its operational-level objective. Nogi's Third Army suffered a further 4,349 casualties, including 924 dead. Russian losses were about 2,800 troops, including 600 dead or missing. From Namako Yama, Japanese forward observers gained a partial view of the Russian warships in the inner harbour. Using a telephone line for fire direction, the Japanese forward observers began spotting for the long-range 12cm and 15cm guns of the Naval Brigade. On 28 September, the battleship *Pobeda* was hit several times, and on 30 September the battleship *Peresvet* was hit nine times. At first, the damage was moderate and the Russian battleships moved to positions behind Quail Hill, which could not be observed. On 1 October, the Japanese managed to set up their first battery of 28cm howitzers near Namako Yama and began firing blindly at the partially hidden Russian warships. On 2 October, the battleship *Peresvet* was hit by nine 28cm shells, which inflicted considerable damage. The 28cm howitzer had two types of shells and it appears that the initial bombardment utilized those filled with black powder, rather than the more destructive Shimosa-filled rounds.

Inside Port Arthur, the garrison was proud that it had weathered two Japanese offensives without ceding too much ground and inflicted better than 2:1 casualties against a numerically superior force. Unlike most sieges, after four months the garrison still had a good stockpile of ammunition, and while the troops were mostly subsisting on rice soup, fish, beans and biscuits, there was no starvation thanks to Togo's ineffective blockade. Small boats were still able to venture out to catch fish in the waters around Port Arthur (despite a nonsensical order from Stoessel forbidding fishing) and blockade runners were able to deliver small cargoes on a regular basis. However, the long-term outlook was less auspicious. The Pacific Fleet was gradually being stripped of sailors and guns

to support the ground battles, while the warships themselves were being rendered inoperative by regular damage from Japanese artillery. On 8 October, another attempt was made to slip a few warships out past the blockade to Vladivostok, when the cruiser *Pallada* and two destroyers sortied. Both destroyers were lost and the *Pallada* returned to Port Arthur, heavily damaged.

News from outside Port Arthur was also distressing. Despite amassing a 2:1 numerical advantage with the main Russian

Japanese dead in a trench at the base of 203-metre Hill. Although the Japanese were able to seize the lower trenches with relative ease, they proved to be death traps, with the Russians on the crest hurling down grenades into them. Note the steep slope in the background. (Author's collection)

army at Liaoyang, Kuropatkin was defeated and forced to retreat on 5 September. The Russian defeat at Liaoyang meant no relief operation by land could be expected before the end of the year, perhaps not until the spring. While it was encouraging to hear that the Tsar was sending the Baltic Fleet to Port Arthur, its warships were also not expected to arrive until early 1905. Consequently, no matter what tactical successes the Port Arthur garrison achieved, by late September the strategic picture indicated that no relief would be likely for at least another six months. Kondratenko wrote a memorandum for Stoessel outlining these factors, which concluded: 'It is hardly possible to count on the timely rescue of Port Arthur by our army or navy.' At great risk, Kondratenko also suggested that Stoessel should recommend to the Tsar to seek peace before the fall of Port Arthur, in order to avoid a national humiliation. Stoessel refused to send any such message to the Tsar, for fear of hurting his career.

On the Japanese side, Nogi was depressed that his first two offensives had failed and that the leadership in Tokyo were already concerned about the great expenditure of lives and ammunition for such small gains. Kodama visited the Third Army during the second offensive and told Nogi to adapt his tactics with more sapping, more artillery bombardments and fewer frontal assaults. Above all else, he stressed the importance of capturing 203-metre Hill as soon as possible. Nogi listened, but he did not accept Kodama's recommendation to concentrate on 203-metre Hill, since he still regarded this position as secondary. Instead, Nogi insisted on making another attempt against the Wantai Heights, as soon as he received more ammunition and infantry replacements. On 1 October, the first 28cm battery was operational, and Nogi ordered his artillery commander to concentrate its fire on the forts on the Wantai Heights. By 15 October, all three batteries of 28cm howitzers were operational. However, Nogi had made a critical error, because the Russians were now afforded over a month to improve their defences around 203-metre Hill without much hindrance from enemy artillery fire.

In late September and early October, both sides began to adapt to trench warfare and adopt tactics that eerily presaged the Western Front of 1915–18. The Japanese engineers introduced body armour and armoured shields, but Russian 37mm QF guns blasted them to pieces. Japanese engineers also tried using smoke screens to get close to barbed-wire obstacles and Bangalore

Nogi's third general assault, 26–30 October 1904

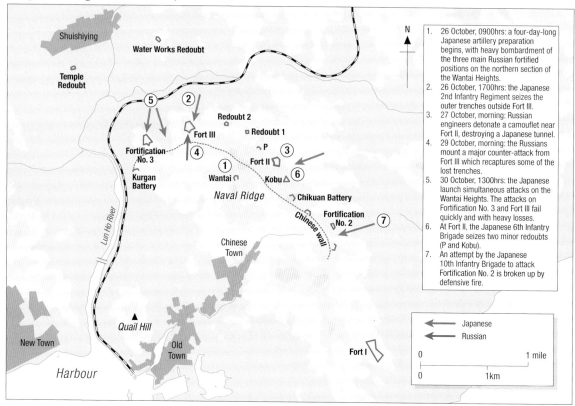

1. 26 October, 0900hrs: a four-day-long Japanese artillery preparation begins, with heavy bombardment of the three main Russian fortified positions on the northern section of the Wantai Heights.
2. 26 October, 1700hrs: the Japanese 2nd Infantry Regiment seizes the outer trenches outside Fort III.
3. 27 October, morning: Russian engineers detonate a camouflet near Fort II, destroying a Japanese tunnel.
4. 29 October, morning: the Russians mount a major counter-attack from Fort III which recaptures some of the lost trenches.
5. 30 October, 1300hrs: the Japanese launch simultaneous attacks on the Wantai Heights. The attacks on Fortification No. 3 and Fort III fail quickly and with heavy losses.
6. At Fort II, the Japanese 6th Infantry Brigade seizes two minor redoubts (P and Kobu).
7. An attempt by the Japanese 10th Infantry Brigade to attack Fortification No. 2 is broken up by defensive fire.

Japanese
Russian

0   1 mile
0   1km

torpedoes to breach them, but the Russians developed mortars to shell these attempts. Japanese saps could advance up to 2–3m in one night, less in rocky terrain. However, the Russians learned to target the 'sap heads' (where most of the engineers were working) with light artillery pieces and their 225mm mine-throwers, which could deliver a devastating explosive charge. Nevertheless, the Japanese engineers worked assiduously above and below ground to get closer to the Russian forts. In particular, great effort was expended tunnelling through solid rock in order to position a mine beneath Fort No. II (Chikuan). However, the Russians detected the tunnelling efforts and began their own counter-mines to disrupt the Japanese operations. Of course, sniping and harassing artillery fire inflicted a steady stream of casualties on the front-line soldiers of both sides.

For his third general offensive, set to begin on 26 October, Nogi intended to use all three divisions (each reduced to roughly 50–55 per cent strength) to capture the key positions on the Wantai Heights: Fortification No. 3 (Sung-shu), Fort III (Ehr-lung) and Fort II. The Russians fully anticipated this course of action and had strengthened their defences along the Chinese Wall, with more sandbags, mines and other obstacles. At 0900hrs on 26 October, the Japanese artillery began its preparation, with emphasis upon Fortification No. 3 and Fort III. The Japanese bombardment would continue intermittently over the next four days, expending approximately 20,000 shells (including 1,800 28cm rounds). All three Russian fortifications were badly damaged, with guns destroyed and heavy personnel casualties. At 1700hrs on 26 October, the Japanese 2nd Infantry Regiment surged forwards and occupied the outer trenches around Fort III, but was then pinned down by heavy Russian defensive fire. Covered by the noise of the bombardment, Japanese engineers accelerated their tunnelling operations towards all three enemy positions. However, the tunnel approaching Fort II was detected, and on the morning of 27 October, the Russians detonated a camouflet which blasted the Japanese engineers to oblivion. On the morning of 29 October, the Russians mounted a major counter-attack from Fort III, and managed to

recover part of the trenches that had been occupied. While Nogi's firepower did serve to degrade the outer Russian defences, it also alerted the Russians to where the main blow would fall. The artillery bombardment was planned to continue until 30 October, when all three Japanese divisions would attack simultaneously at 1300hrs.

In a scene that would be repeated at Gallipoli in 1915 and on the Somme in 1916, the Japanese barrage lifted just before 1300hrs, and then roughly 20,000 Japanese troops in five assault regiments surged forwards from their saps and trenches. The Russian line was held by 26 companies, with perhaps 3,000 infantry and 500 gunners. In some places, the distance between the saps and the forward Russian positions was as little as 40m. Yet, it was enough. The 2nd Infantry Regiment attacked Fortification No. 3 and managed to reach the outer trenches, but then discovered that the moat around the fort was deeper than expected and their ladders were too short. The same thing happened with the Japanese 19th Infantry Regiment attack on Fort III. With the Japanese infantry stopped by the moat, the Russian defenders raked them with point-blank cannister and machine-gun fire, causing the attackers to recoil in disorder. The 9th Infantry Division had a little more luck in the fight for Fort II. Although Ichinohe's 6th Infantry Brigade failed to capture the main fort, it did seize two minor positions (P Redoubt and Kobu) on either side of the fort. Russian counter-attacks threatened to eliminate both toeholds, but Ichinohe personally ensured the hard-won terrain was held. On the left flank, the 10th Infantry Brigade tried to attack Fortification No. 2 (the Chikuan battery) but its formations were broken up by Russian artillery fire. By late afternoon of 30 October, it was clear that Nogi's third general offensive had failed. Indeed, the repulse of this assault was probably the biggest Russian tactical victory in the campaign.

Altogether, Nogi's Third Army suffered a further 3,874 casualties (including 1,092 dead) in the offensive and captured no major positions. The tiny footholds that had been gained on the Wantai Heights were costly to hold and difficult to supply. In comparison, the Russians suffered 5,069 casualties (including 616 dead). As of 1 November, the Russians still had 26,559 combat troops (including 1,850 sailors, 5,625 artillerymen and 1,165 auxiliary troops), but their ammunition situation was becoming precarious.

Japanese lightly wounded personnel recovering behind the lines. Nogi's Third Army was not provided with adequate medical support units to deal with tens of thousands of battle casualties and troops sick from various diseases. (Author's collection)

The Russians have stacked piles of dead Japanese soldiers near 203-metre Hill. Nogi's Third Army suffered over 10,000 casualties around this one position, which was shocking for officers trained in 19th-century manoeuvre warfare theory. (Author's collection)

Most of the Russian heavy artillery had very little ammunition left, and the field guns had expended about two-thirds of their stockpile, although there were still plenty of small-caliber rounds available. Consequently, the Russian artillery was now forced to limit its firing to repelling assaults and could no longer engage in counter-battery missions. Disease was starting to become a factor in undermining the garrison as well, as the limited diet led to scurvy and other maladies. Inside Port Arthur, the mood was growing increasingly grim, despite the successful repulse of the third general offensive. News that Kuropatkin had suffered another major defeat in the Battle of the Shaho ended any hope that the Russian army in Manchuria would relieve the siege of Port Arthur. The Russian Baltic Fleet had left its home ports on 15 October, but it would not be in a position to render any material assistance to the garrison in Port Arthur for many months, if ever. Nevertheless, the garrison continued to improve its defences and hope for an honourable exit from the war, rather than ignominious defeat. Winter weather had arrived, with freezing temperatures (~25° F) adding to the misery of life in the front-line trenches.

THE SIEGE REACHES ITS CLIMAX

While the Russian defences on the Wantai Heights were not impregnable, they were strong enough to frustrate the kind of brute-force tactics that Nogi was employing. In Tokyo, officers in the Imperial General Staff advocated a shift in focus towards 203-metre Hill instead of continuing to pound on the Wantai Heights. The leadership of the IJN also advocated this approach, since the seizure of this hill would provide the unobstructed visibility into the harbour required to destroy the Russian fleet. In order to accomplish this objective, the General Staff decided to send the 7th Infantry Division

to reinforce Nogi's Third Army. However, Nogi attached little importance to the navy's opinion about where he should be attacking and steadfastly decided to mount another attempt on the Wantai Heights, which would be a virtual repeat of his failed third offensive. In a sign of how desperate the Third Army was becoming after three failed offensives, Major-General Nakamura Satoru suggested to Nogi to form a 'special reserve unit' (*Shirodasukitai*) as a type of forlorn hope to ensure the capture of at least one of the Russian forts. Nogi agreed and put Nakamura in charge of

Initial phase of the Japanese fourth general assault, 26–29 November 1904

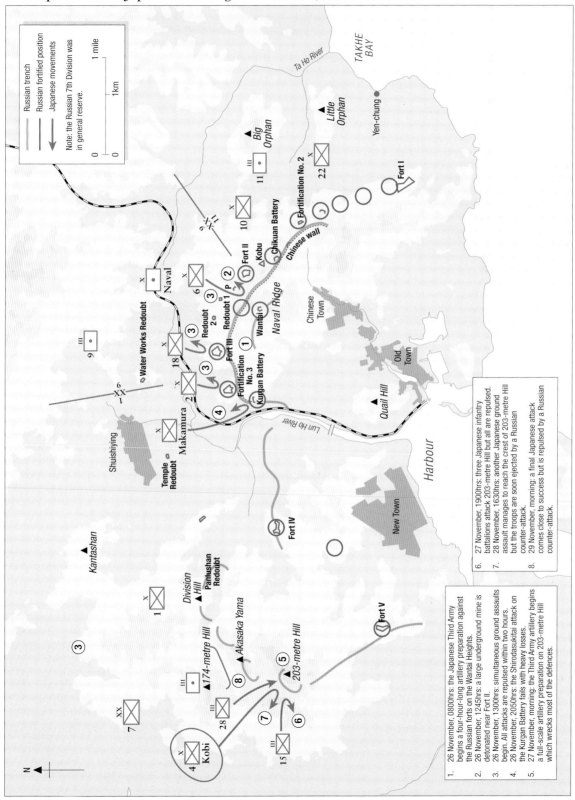

Legend:
- Russian trench
- Russian fortified position
- Japanese movements
- Note: the Russian 7th Division was in general reserve.

1 mile
1km

TAKHE BAY

Ta Ho River

Yen-chung
Little Orphan
Big Orphan
Fort I
Fortification No. 2
Chinese wall
Chikuan Battery
Kobu
Fort II
Naval Ridge
Naval Redoubt
Water Works Redoubt
Redoubt 2
Redoubt 1
Wantai
Fort III
Fortification No. 3
Kurgan Battery
Chinese Town
Old Town
Quail Hill
Makamura
Temple Redoubt
Shuishiying
Harbour
Lun Ho River
New Town
Fort IV
Kantashan
Panlushan Redoubt
Division Hill
Akasaka Yama
174-metre Hill
203-metre Hill
Fort V
Kobi

N

1. 26 November, 0800hrs: the Japanese Third Army begins a four-hour-long artillery preparation against the Russian forts on the Wantai Heights.
2. 26 November, 1245hrs: a large underground mine is detonated near Fort II.
3. 26 November, 1300hrs: simultaneous ground assaults begin. All attacks are repulsed within two hours.
4. 26 November, 2050hrs: the Shirodasukitai attack on the Kurgan Battery fails with heavy losses.
5. 27 November, morning: the Third Army artillery begins a full-scale artillery preparation on 203-metre Hill which wrecks most of the defences.
6. 27 November, 1900hrs: three Japanese infantry battalions attack 203-metre Hill but all are repulsed.
7. 28 November, 1630hrs: another Japanese ground assault manages to reach the crest of 203-metre Hill but the troops are soon ejected by a Russian counter-attack.
8. 29 November, morning: a final Japanese attack comes close to success but is repulsed by a Russian counter-attack.

75

The Japanese detonated a large mine next to Fort II on 26 November 1904, at the start of the fourth general offensive. Note the communication trenches leading up the slope. Despite the size of the explosion, the mine did not inflict sufficient damage, and the Japanese infantry assault was repulsed. (Author's collection)

the brigade-size formation, which consisted of battalions from all four Japanese infantry divisions.

At 0800hrs on 26 November, Nogi began his fourth general offensive with a four-hour-long artillery bombardment against the main forts on the Wantai Heights. The Japanese artillery, particularly the 28cm howitzers, inflicted considerable damage on the Russian forts, although the garrisons hunkered down inside bomb-proof shelters. Just prior to the ground assault, the Japanese detonated a large mine near Fort II, but it did not inflict much damage.

At 1300hrs, the 1st, 9th and 11th Infantry divisions mounted regimental-size assaults on the Russian forts to their front, but immediately ran into a hail of rifle, machine-gun and cannister fire. Although some Japanese troops reached the parapets at Fort II, they were quickly killed. Within two hours, all the Japanese assaults had been repulsed with heavy losses. Despite this failure, Nakamura convinced Nogi to authorize a night attack by his *Shirodasukitai*. At dusk, Nakamura led his unit through dead space to the west of Fortification No. 3, towards the Kurgan Battery. The Japanese soldiers wore white tape on their uniforms, for identification in the dark. By 2050hrs, Nakamura's column had stealthily managed to reach the Kurgan Battery when it was suddenly detected. Russian searchlights snapped on, spotlighting the Japanese troops in the open, followed seconds later by a storm of shrapnel fire. Amazingly, a few Japanese troops fought their way into the battery, but three companies of Russian sailors quickly arrived to lead a violent counter-attack. Nakamura was wounded and his brigade shattered by heavy losses, so he ordered a retreat. The *Shirodasukitai*, an early form of banzai attack, had failed, suffering 45 per cent casualties in the process.

Altogether, the Japanese attacks on 26 November had cost the Third Army a further 4,500 casualties for no gains. By this point, it was clear even to Nogi's heedless command style that continued attacks on the Wantai Heights were unlikely to succeed, so he finally agreed to shift focus back to 203-metre Hill. However, Nogi had given Tretyakov a vital month in which to complete the fortification of this key position. By late November, Tretyakov's troops had completed two strong redoubts on the twin crests (203m and 210m in height), surrounded by barbed wire and a 2m-deep trench. The garrison consisted of five infantry companies (2., 4. and 6./5th East Siberian Rifle Regiment; 7./14th East Siberian Rifle Regiment; and 1./27th East Siberian Rifle Regiment), a detachment of sailors and four machine guns. On the nearby Akasaka Yama (180-metre Hill), which was connected to 203-metre Hill by communications trenches, Kondratenko had deployed the bulk of the 27th East Siberian Rifle Regiment. The Russians had also laid telephone wire to the top of 203-metre Hill, so Tretyakov could be instantly apprised of enemy activity.

On the evening of 26 November, the Japanese artillery began a preparation against 203-metre Hill, firing 25 28cm shells and about 300 lighter-caliber rounds. In response, Tretyakov raised his troops to full readiness and moved up his reserves to nearby positions. The next morning, the Japanese artillery began a much larger bombardment; Tretyakov later wrote that '203-metre Hill resembled a volcano in eruption'. The left redoubt on the crest was badly damaged and the telephone links were broken. Tretyakov estimated that the hill was hit by a further 30 28cm shells and about 300 15cm shells. By late afternoon, the Russian positions atop 203-metre Hill were badly battered, and Nogi ordered the 1st Infantry Division to send in its men. Around 1900hrs, two battalions from the 15th Infantry Regiment attacked the south-west corner of the hill while one battalion from the 38th Reserve Infantry Regiment (4th Kobi Brigade) attacked the centre of the hill. Despite the pounding that they had received, the Russian garrison repulsed both attacks. On 28 November, the Japanese resumed their bombardment, followed by another infantry assault by two regiments at 1630hrs; this time, some troops from the 16th Reserve Infantry Regiment reached the crest. Tretyakov immediately organized a counter-attack which drove out the Japanese by 1900hrs. Before dawn on 29 November, Japanese infantrymen crept close to the upper trench line on 203-metre-Hill and hurled a volley of grenades into it, which sparked a brief panic. However, Tretyakov was on hand, and he personally rallied his soldiers before the Japanese could capture the redoubt. A quick counter-attack with the bayonet eliminated the Japanese raiders. After this attack, the Japanese 1st Infantry Division lacked the strength for further offensive operations. While the Russian troops had put up a magnificent defence of 203-metre Hill, the troops were exhausted by three days of continuous bombardment and attacks. Tretyakov had been wounded (he remained on the hill) and was running out of reserves to replace losses. Irmanov had no further reserves to give Tretyakov because Japanese probing attacks on nearby Akasaka Yama also required atention; if either position was lost, the Russian defence in this sector would fold.

Nogi threw in his last card – Lieutenant-General Osako Naotoshi's fresh 7th Infantry Division – which was assigned to capture 203-metre Hill. Yet rather than maintain unity of command and allow Osako to run the operation,

A memorial to General Kondratenko, at the site of where he was killed. The monument was erected during the Japanese occupation of the city, but is still maintained by the Chinese Government as part of the remains of Fort II. (Author's collection)

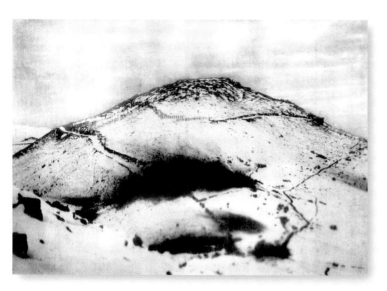

203-metre Hill, after its capture, seen from the south-west in December 1904. The double rows of barbed-wire obstacles are quite clear in this photo, as well as some of the trenches near the crest. Extremely steep and devoid of any cover, 203-metre Hill required an extreme level of effort to capture.

he was obliged to provide his infantry and artillery to General Tsumumoto (1st Infantry Division commander), who created a composite formation from multiple units. At 0600hrs on 30 November, the Japanese artillery resumed its bombardment of 203-metre Hill, including two cruisers firing from near Louisa Bay, west of Port Arthur. Soon afterwards, another infantry ground assault commenced. The troops from the 28th Infantry Regiment were able to seize part of the north-west corner of the hill, but were pinned down by Russian fire. Another Japanese attack at 2040hrs actually succeeded in capturing the redoubt on the northern crest, but Tretyakov organized a counter-attack with his last few reserves to retake it with hand grenades at 0200hrs. During the night fighting around 203-metre Hill, Nogi's younger son, Second Lieutenant Nogi Yasunori, was killed by Russian artillery fire. Adding to the Japanese list of misfortunes, the protected cruiser *Sai Yen* was sunk by a Russian mine off Louisa Bay; following this incident, Togo refused to risk any more of his warships on naval gunfire support missions. After four days of costly failures, Nogi decided to postpone any further attacks on 203-metre Hill until he could reorganize his infantry and artillery.

Nogi did keep the pressure on 203-metre Hill and the adjoining Akasaka Yama, while preparing for a larger assault. The Japanese 28cm howitzers destroyed the redoubts and trenches atop the hill, although the Russian troops used sandbags to keep building new fortified positions. Russian sailors and non-combat personnel were increasingly assigned to refill the depleted garrison, which was suffering heavy losses to the artillery bombardments. On the evening of 4 December, Tretyakov himself was badly wounded by artillery fire. At 1400hrs on 5 December, the 7th Infantry Division attacked the south-west corner of 203-metre Hill, now defended by just two reduced-strength companies. The Japanese infantry were able to reach the crest, but were counter-attacked by the remaining Russian troops, who were virtually leaderless. After intense close-quarter fighting on the summit, the remaining Russians fell back, and by 1700hrs two Japanese battalions held the top of the hill. The Japanese quickly consolidated on their objective by hauling several Hotchkiss machine guns up to reinforce their worn-out assault troops. 203-metre Hill had been conquered by the Japanese 28cm siege guns.

Kondratenko lacked the reserves to recover 203-metre Hill, and once it was lost, the decision was made to evacuate Akasaka Yama and Division Hill, as well. These three positions were essentially a package deal, and from 203-metre Hill the Japanese could make communications with the other two hills very difficult. By shortening the line, Kondratenko had a better chance of holding the final inner line with his remaining infantry. Nogi's fourth general offensive had been a bruising affair for both sides. The Third Army suffered 16,936 casualties (including 5,052 dead) compared with 17,380

Russian casualties (including 5,380 dead). As soon as the Japanese could install forward observers on 203-metre Hill, they redirected their 28cm howitzer batteries to begin shelling the fleet in the inner harbour, which lay less than 6km away. By this point, most of the Russian warships only had skeleton crews remaining aboard. On the afternoon of 5 December, the battleship *Poltava* was hit and one of its magazines exploded, causing it to sink in shallow water. On 6 December, the battleship *Retvizan* was sunk by 14 28cm shells, and the next day the battleship *Pobeda* was sunk. The cruisers *Pallada* and *Bayan* were sunk on 8–9 December. In an effort to deceive the Japanese, the Russians scuttled the battleship *Peresvet* in very shallow water to make it appear sunk. The only battleship to survive the bombardment was Captain Nikolai von Essen's *Sevastopol*, which moved outside the inner harbour on the night of 8 December and anchored in the small White Wolf Bay, just below the 6in. guns of coastal battery No. 2. The Russians emplaced anti-torpedo nets and floating booms around the battleship to protect it from Japanese torpedo boats, and the remaining small warships of the fleet (seven destroyers and the gunboat *Otvazhnyy*) deployed around her in a screen.

Togo concentrated on destroying the cornered *Sevastopol*, while Nogi focused on completing his siege operations against the remaining Russian positions on the Wantai Heights. On 8 December, the senior Russian officers held a council of war in Port Arthur; Kondratenko and Smirnov advocated continuing to fight until supplies were exhausted, whereas Stoessel and Fok were quietly in favour of capitulation. Kondratenko argued that with 20,000 troops and a month's stockpile of food and ammunition still available, it was inappropriate to be discussing surrender. The garrison still had the ability to inflict significant losses on the enemy and to delay their strategic timetable, which would benefit the larger Russian war effort. No decision was reached. Four days later, a British steamer made it through Togo's porous blockade with 800 tons of cargo, including food, which temporarily raised spirits. However, the death of General Kondratenko while inspecting Fort II on the evening of 15 December seriously shook morale. With Kondratenko dead and Tretyakov seriously wounded, as well as the loss of many other front-line leaders, the Russian defence became flaccid. Soldiers lived in their frozen trenches, gnawing on horsemeat, waiting for the end.

Outside the port, Togo was eager to end the blockade so his ships could return to refit at Sasebo prior to the expected arrival of the Russian Baltic Fleet (which would soon reach the Indian Ocean). Although most of the Russian Pacific Squadron was sitting on the muddy bottom of Port Arthur's inner harbour, Russian coastal defences continued to inflict losses on Togo's fleet. On 13 December, the cruiser *Takasago* struck a Russian mine, and the resulting magazine explosion killed 273 of her crew. The battleship *Sevastopol* was beyond the range of Nogi's 28cm howitzers, but Togo tried to shell it with long-range naval gunfire. When this failed, he decided on the desperate expedient of sending torpedo boats and destroyers to attack the battleship directly with torpedoes, which meant passage through mined waters. On the night of 9 December, Togo's torpedo boats made their first attempt to attack the *Sevastopol*, which failed. Undeterred, five more attempts were made between 11 and 15 December. Captain Nikolai von Essen's battleship put up stiff resistance, aided by his escort vessels, the coastal batteries and plenty of mines. The Japanese destroyers and torpedo boats fired off about

THE DEATH OF GENERAL KONDRATENKO, 15 DECEMBER 1904 (PP. 80–81)

General-leytenant Roman I. Kondratenko, commander of the 7th East Siberian Rifle Division, provided the heart and soul of the defence of Port Arthur. Throughout the siege, Kondratenko was a dynamic front-line leader who instilled the will to fight among his troops – if not in his superiors. He was often in forward positions, directing repairs and organizing counter-attacks, as necessary. As an engineer, Kondratenko was also a tactical innovator, who encouraged his troops to develop new booby-traps and improvised weapons in order to inflict maximum losses on the enemy. He formed his personal staff from capable, like-minded officers, often engineers such as himself. Yet Kondratenko was also something of an anomaly among the senior Russian leaders at Port Arthur, and hence irreplaceable.

On the afternoon of 15 December 1904, Kondratenko and his staff went to Fort No. 2 on the eastern heights, to inspect the condition of its garrison. The fort had already been badly battered by Japanese howitzer fire, but was still capable of resistance. Kondratenko took the opportunity to award medals to several troops for bravery, and to meet with the garrison commander. Shortly after 2000hrs, the Japanese began shelling Fort No. 2 with a battery of their 28cm (11in.) howitzers, so Kondratenko and his staff took shelter within one of the fort's casemates. At 2015hrs, one of the 217kg shells hit and penetrated the casemate, killing Kondratenko and eight other officers. Seven other officers were badly wounded.

In this scene, moments after the impact, Kondratenko (**1**) is already dead or dying. Russian staff officers (**2**) are lying next to him in the ruins of the casement, which has a gaping hole in its ceiling. Smoke and debris fill the air within the shattered casemate. Nogi's artillery fired over 353,000 rounds during the siege, but this one 28cm round proved to have the greatest impact. Russian front-line morale, already tenuous, plummeted once it was learned that Kondratenko and most of his staff were eliminated. With Kondratenko dead, General Stoessel no longer faced serious opposition to his intent to surrender the fortress, and all resistance would collapse in less than two weeks.

80 torpedoes without achieving any success due to the anti-torpedo nets, but lost two torpedo boats sunk (*No. 42* and *No. 53*) and six destroyers damaged. Finally, on the night of 15 December, the Japanese managed to score a single hit on *Sevastopol*'s stern, which disabled its steering. Von Essen decided to maintain his ship as a floating battery for the time being, but ordered the remaining six operational destroyers to make a dash for neutral ports on the night of 19/20 December. All six destroyers succeed in breaking out – again indicating the porous nature of the Japanese blockade – with four reaching Chefu (Yantai) and two German-held Qingdao. All six destroyers were interned, but later returned to Russian control. With the last elements of the Pacific Squadron eliminated, most of Togo's Combined Fleet returned home to refit and await the arrival of the Russian Baltic Fleet.

As soon as the Japanese occupied 203-metre Hill, they set up an artillery forward-observer position on the summit to direct the fire of their 28cm howitzers against the Russian warships in the inner harbour. (Author's collection)

After the death of Kondratenko, Stoessel installed Fok as commander of the ground defence, overriding the objections of Smirnov. Fok immediately ordered Gorbatovsky, still in command on the Wantai Heights, to thin out his front-line garrisons in order to reduce casualties and to conserve artillery ammunition. Consequently, Nogi's engineers were given nearly free rein to advance their saps and tunnels with much less interference from the Russians. At 1300hrs on 18 December, the Japanese detonated a 2,000kg charge underneath Fort II (Chikuan), which collapsed the central parapet. Assault troops from the 11th Infantry Division moved rapidly to exploit the breach, but the Russian garrison – now just 150 troops – put up stiff resistance and inflicted heavy casualties. Russian machine-gun fire and shrapnel rounds prevented the Japanese from moving more troops into the ruins of the fort, and eventually the Russian garrison eliminated the assault group. Altogether, the Russians suffered 92 killed in action but inflicted 699 casualties on the Japanese. Gorbatovsky appealed for reserves to replace the fought-out garrison, but instead Fok ordered him to evacuate Fort II. Gorbatovsky tried to ignore him, but Fok passed a direct order to the officer in charge of the garrison to evacuate the fort, which was obeyed. Thus, Fort II was lost. On 19 December, Gorbatovsky also tried to deploy reserves to save the Eagle's Nest position in the second line of defence, but Fok overruled him and ordered it evacuated. Fok's erratic decision-making proved to be a wrecking ball for any local attempts to salvage threatened front-line positions.

Nogi now shifted to the reduction of Fort III and Fortification No. 3. Japanese tunnelling efforts moved into high gear, and on the morning of 28 December, a dozen underground charges were detonated beneath Fort III (Erhlung), destroying most of the structure and killing half the 300-man garrison. However, the Japanese 9th Infantry Division waited two hours before launching an assault, which gave the fort's commander, Kapitan Bulgakov, a chance to reorganize the survivors. The Russians poured machine-gun fire and cannister rounds from quick-firing guns into the attackers at the breach, inflicting heavy losses. Gorbatovsky was able to send two companies of reserves to bolster the garrison, which prolonged the fight, but eventually the Japanese outflanked the ruins of the fort. Bulgakov decided to evacuate

Final operations around Port Arthur, 5–31 December 1904

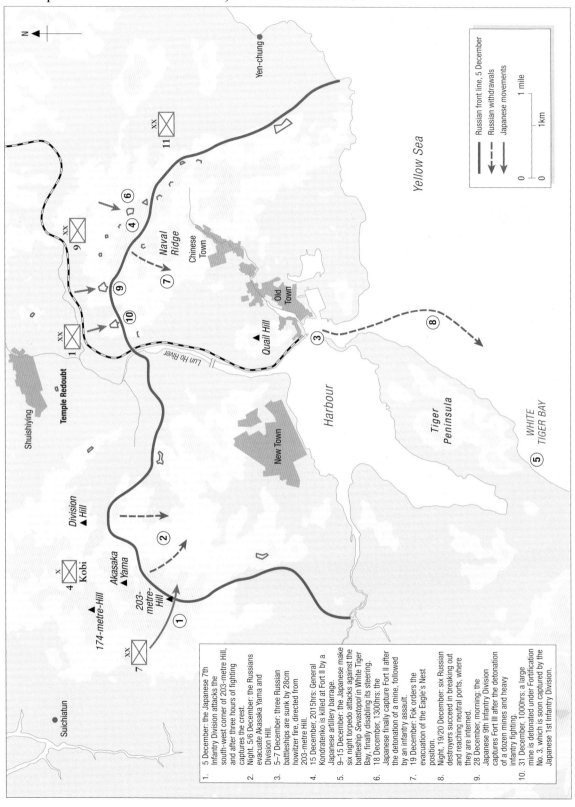

Legend:
- Russian front line, 5 December
- Russian withdrawals
- Japanese movements

0 ———— 1 mile
0 ———— 1km

1. 5 December: the Japanese 7th Infantry Division attacks the south-west corner of 203-metre Hill, and after three hours of fighting captures the crest.
2. Night, 5/6 December: the Russians evacuate Akasaka Yama and Division Hill.
3. 5–7 December: three Russian battleships are sunk by 28cm howitzer fire, directed from 203-metre Hill.
4. 15 December, 2015hrs: General Kondratenko is killed at Fort II by a Japanese artillery barrage.
5. 9–15 December: the Japanese make six night torpedo attacks against the battleship *Sevastopol* in White Tiger Bay, finally disabling its steering.
6. 18 December, 1300hrs: the Japanese finally capture Fort II after the detonation of a mine, followed by an infantry assault.
7. 19 December: Fok orders the evacuation of the Eagle's Nest position.
8. Night, 19/20 December: six Russian destroyers succeed in breaking out and reaching neutral ports, where they are interned.
9. 28 December, morning: the Japanese 9th Infantry Division captures Fort III after the detonation of a dozen mines and heavy infantry fighting.
10. 31 December, 1000hrs: a large mine is detonated under Fortification No. 3, which is soon captured by the Japanese 1st Infantry Division.

The Chinese Government has installed a number of historical markers on 203-metre Hill, in several languages. This plaque marks the spot where the Russian command post on 203-metre Hill was located. (Author's collection)

the ruins before his troops were cut off, but they had succeeded in inflicting 1,190 casualties on the attackers (including 237 dead).

After the loss of Fort III, Stoessel opted to hold another council of war on 29 December, although he had already made up his mind to seek terms from Nogi. Of 22 officers present, only Stoessel, Fok and three others recommended capitulation, against the majority which favoured continued resistance. No decisions were announced, but Stoessel had already drafted a letter of capitulation. Fortification No. 3 was obviously the next target for the Japanese sappers and Fok forced Gorbatovsky to reduce the garrison to just 208 troops. At 1000hrs on 31 December, the Japanese detonated a mine under the fortification, which killed nearly half the garrison. Denied reinforcements by Fok, the remainder of the garrison fought until overwhelmed by 1100hrs. The final capture of this position was a relatively cheap triumph for the 1st Infantry Division, which suffered just 187 casualties (including 18 dead). In an act that can only be described as criminal stupidity, Fok ordered all five remaining reserve companies to fall back to New Town, leaving Gorbatovsky with just 45 soldiers as a reserve for the remaining positions along the Chinese Wall.

On the morning of 1 January 1905, Nogi's Third Army began to advance against the Chinese Wall, which they now recognized was only lightly defended. Russian resistance began to evaporate and the village of Wantai was soon occupied. Without informing Smirnov or any other senior officer, Stoessel dispatched a staff officer under a flag of truce, bearing the letter requesting terms from Nogi. Stoessel also sent one last message to the Tsar, claiming that, 'we have hardly any ammunition left. I have now 10,000 men under arms. They are all ill.' Nogi was surprised to receive a request for terms when the Russian innermost defences were still intact, but he agreed to a meeting. At 1100hrs on 2 January, Nogi and Stoessel met in the village of Shuishiying. After some haggling on terms, Stoessel finally signed the capitulation document by dusk, thereby surrendering Port Arthur to Nogi's Third Army. When news of the surrender was announced, many Russian troops began looting in Port Arthur, particularly alcohol, and there was a breakdown in discipline. Some Russian officers asked permission to try to escape in any remaining vessels in order to join up with Kuropatkin's army, but Stoessel forbade it.

Altogether, over 41,000 Russian military personnel went into captivity (including 8,956 sailors), of whom about 5,000 were sick and 8,000 wounded. Of the 168 senior Russian officers in Port Arthur, 86 accepted parole from the Japanese, including Stoessel, General-mayor Viktor Reis and General-mayor Mitrofan Nadein. A total of 357 artillery pieces and nine machine guns were captured intact, indicating heavy losses of weaponry in the final actions. The Japanese were surprised to discover that Port Arthur still had significant stocks of ammunition (including 2.2 million rounds of small-arms ammunition and 133,000 artillery shells) and food (roughly 30 days' worth). Indeed, the garrison still had 1,920 horses, indicating that the troops were not starving. Contrary to what Stoessel told the Tsar, the garrison still possessed more than 20,000 able-bodied troops and enough material resources to fight on for at least another 4–6 weeks. Given the presence of foreign correspondents and Japan's need for foreign loans to continue the war, the Japanese treated their Russian prisoners according to the terms of the 1899 Hague Convention. Several prisoner-of-war camps were established in the Nagasaki area and elsewhere. All of the Russian prisoners would be repatriated after the peace treaty was signed eight months later. After spending two weeks at Nagasaki, Stoessel and several of his senior officers were sent home via the French mail steamer *Australien*; he arrived in the Crimea on 21 February and met with the Tsar in St Petersburg on 3 March. Initially, Stoessel was acclaimed a hero and decorated by the Tsar, but once the truth started trickling out, he was placed under house arrest.

The eight-month-long Port Arthur campaign cost Nogi's Third Army approximately 59,400 casualties (including 15,400 dead), equivalent to almost 40 per cent of the troops allocated to the operation. In addition, the protracted siege consumed 353,065 rounds of artillery ammunition, which reduced the level of artillery support for other IJA operations in Manchuria. Indeed, the siege of Port Arthur, with Nogi's fruitless general offensives, ended up being a sinkhole that diverted a great deal of Japanese resources away from the main theatre of operations. After the capture of Port Arthur, Nogi's Third Army was able to head northwards and join the main Japanese army group in time for the decisive Battle of Mukden in February 1905. Togo's Combined Fleet lost two battleships, three cruisers, one coast defence ship and several torpedo boats in the waters around Port Arthur, as well as over 1,500 sailors (in contrast, Togo lost only three torpedo boats and 117 sailors killed at the Battle of Tsushima). While Port Arthur ended in a Japanese victory, it was a costly one, particularly for an operation that was intended to be secondary in importance to the main campaign in southern Manchuria.

The Russians suffered roughly 30,000 casualties during the Port Arthur campaign, including about 16,000 dead. The entire III Siberian Rifle Corps was lost at Port Arthur, although by that point Kuropatkin had amassed 12 other rifle corps in Manchuria. The Russian Pacific Squadron was virtually destroyed as a result of the campaign and the pitiful remnant would remain an anaemic, non-threatening coastal defence force for the next 40 years. After the fall of Port Arthur, Russian plans for expansion in East Asia lay in ruins.

AFTERMATH

The Russians failed to fully demolish their sunk or immobilized warships in Port Arthur, which enabled the Japanese to eventually salvage four battleships and three cruisers. These warships served in the IJN for over a decade, although the battleships *Persevet* and *Poltava* were sold back to Russia in 1916. The one battleship, two cruisers and ten destroyers that were interned in neutral ports all returned to active Russian service immediately after the war. Port Arthur itself became a Japanese military base for the next 40 years, redesignated as the Ryojun Naval District, although the IJN made very little use of the facility. Indeed, the main use of Ryojun was to be the home port for a minesweeper flotilla that spent years clearing the surrounding waters of mines laid around the port. By the 1920s, the naval base was in caretaker status and remained that way throughout World War II. At the close of that war, General-leytenant Vladimir D. Ivanov and 204 soldiers flew into Port Arthur on American-built C-47 transports on 22 August 1945 to take the surrender of the Japanese garrison. Ivanov told the Japanese commander that, '40 years ago, General Stoessel surrendered Port Arthur, and now we retook it and we will never leave here again!' Although the Soviets kept Port Arthur for the next decade, Premier Nikita Khrushchev decided to hand the base back to the People's Republic of China in 1956.

The sunken battleships *Persevet* and *Poltava* in the inner harbour, after the surrender of Port Arthur. Amazingly, the Japanese were able to salvage most of the Russian capital ships and integrate them into their own fleet. (Author's collection)

The fall of Port Arthur proved to be a national disaster for Tsarist Russia, which was followed up by Kuropatkin's defeat at the Battle of Mukden in February 1905 and the annihilation of the Baltic Fleet by Togo at the Battle of Tsushima in May 1905. Military defeat served as an accelerant for the outbreak of revolution in Russia, which threatened the stability of the regime. The pre-war decisions to build up the Russian naval presence at Port Arthur and risk war with Japan over spheres of influence in Manchuria and Korea now became clear folly, as Sergei Witte had predicted.

Vice Admiral Yevgeni I. Alekseyev, who played such a large role in setting the stage for the Russian disaster at Port Arthur, was relieved of command, but was soon granted a seat on the State Council. After the peace treaty with Japan was signed in September 1905, the Russian Imperial Army began to examine the Port Arthur campaign in great detail, particularly the decisions that led to capitulation. Smirnov, who had been so acquiescent in Port Arthur, aggressively led the charge in pointing out Stoessel, Fok and Reis as the primary authors of defeat. Stoessel was dismissed from the army in 1906, but then court-martialed in 1908. The court found Stoessel guilty of cowardice and a variety of other charges, which led to a death sentence. After serving a year in prison, Stoessel was pardoned by the Tsar. Fok wounded Smirnov in a duel, but was dismissed from the army and went to Bulgaria. Reis was also dismissed from the army. Smirnov was acquitted of any wrongdoing at Port Arthur, but retired from the army and went to Yugoslavia. Tretyakov was recognized as one of the heroes of Port Arthur and continued to serve in the Russian Army as an engineer until 1917, when he died of pneumonia. Gorbatovsky, another hero of the siege, rose to be an army commander in World War I.

On the Japanese side, Nogi was acclaimed as the victor at Port Arthur, but he was also ashamed of the heavy casualties the Third Army had suffered. When he met the Emperor in Tokyo, he apologized for losing so many troops and requested permission to commit suicide. The Emperor Meiji refused this request, but Nogi later committed suicide after the emperor's death in 1912. Admiral Togo was lionized by the British press after his victory at the Battle of Tsushima, and enjoyed widespread acclaim both at home and abroad until his death in 1934. However, he did not apologize for the heavy losses his fleet suffered in the Port Arthur campaign, nor the mistakes he made during the blockade operations. Despite the failure of his *Shirodasukitai* attack, Nakamura Satoru continued to rise in the IJA after Port Arthur, and ended up with a seat on the Supreme War Council by 1917. Ichinohe Hyoe, who played a critical role in

At the moment of surrender, Japanese troops arrive to replace Russian sentries in one of the forward command posts. Note the long line of disarmed Russian troops in the background. Given the brutal ferocity of fighting during the siege, the moment of surrender was marked by a surprising level of decorum by both sides. (Author's collection)

the Third Army gaining a foothold on the Wantai Heights, enjoyed a successful career in the IJA, and also joined the Supreme War Council in 1917. Interestingly, very little recognition went to the infantry officers directly involved with the costly fighting around 203-metre Hill, or the artillerymen and engineers who actually won the campaign for Japan.

ANALYSIS

The Port Arthur campaign was the first modern siege because a wide variety of new equipment and tactics were employed, breaking away from previous methods of warfare. Even contemporary observers noted that the combination of machine guns, quick-firing artillery, barbed wire and trenches gave an enormous advantage to the defence. The cost of mounting massed infantry attacks across open terrain against this type of defence was prohibitively costly, and Nogi found himself decimating his own regiments and brigades just to achieve minor gains. While the Japanese heavy 28cm siege guns could blast any position into rubble, as long as the defenders were willing to keep feeding reserves in to replace losses and stack more sandbags, the position could usually be held. At Port Arthur, God was not always on the side of the bigger battalions, but on the side with the most determination. Furthermore, the constant presence of the enemy in nearby trenches and saps – often hurling hand grenades throughout the day – quickly exhausted front-line troops. Local commanders had to become very judicious in recognizing when it was time to relieve decimated units, before they became combat ineffective. The see-saw fighting over positions such as 203-metre Hill led to concentrated devastation over small areas of front, which became blood-soaked killing grounds. As a result, a new type of intense, protracted, positional warfare was demonstrated for the first time at Port Arthur – with brute force and firepower becoming the primary arbiters, rather than manoeuvre. Interestingly, the tactical problems of 1904 – such as how to break a well-defended trench line or how to hold one against an enemy equipped with heavy howitzers – were left unanswered. For the most part, foreign military observers saw these new conditions, but then went home and did not consider them apropos until they reappeared on the battlefields of 1914–15.

The senior leadership on both sides in the Port Arthur campaign was abominable. Professional ignorance and pig-headedness are certainly not desirable characteristics in generals, but Nogi and Stoessel actively worked to undermine the best efforts of their subordinates. Nogi did not understand modern warfare, and proved unwilling to learn. Tactical innovation and cooperation with the navy were anathema to him. Instead, he preferred simplistic brute-force solutions, but could not understand why his frontal attacks kept failing. Nogi was fortunate in that the General Staff continued to provide him with replacements and ammunition, otherwise his campaign would have ground to an ignominious halt by October 1904. Stoessel's level of military incompetence seemed to increase as Nogi's Third Army approached Port Arthur. Initially he delegated combat decision-making to Fok and Kondratenko, preferring to focus on minor administrative issues, but by November he could no longer avoid the battle. Although Stoessel was made the primary scapegoat for the capitulation of Port Arthur, it was

Dejected Russian sailors march into captivity. The prisoners were marched to Dalny, where they embarked for POW camps in Japan. (Author's collection)

Fok's persistent effort to deny the release of reserves which led to the loss of one key position after another. Thus, it is no great leap of imagination to suggest that if Stoessel had obeyed the Tsar's order to turn over his command to Smirnov and then Fok was relieved of command, the Russian tactical situation at Port Arthur could only have improved. With better leadership, the Russian garrison would likely have held out longer and inflicted greater losses on the enemy – which at the very least would have prevented Nogi's Third Army from participating in the Battle of Mukden. While the fate of Port Arthur was decided by the earlier Battle of Liaoyang and the Pacific Squadron's unwillingness to contest the waters around the Liaodong Peninsula, the Russian garrison did possess the ability to seriously upset Japan's strategic timetable.

On the Japanese side, Togo's failure to plan for a tight blockade ensured that the garrison would not be starved out, and allowed portions of the Russian squadron in Port Arthur to escape to neutral internment. The Russian Navy's preference for reliance on mine warfare was cost-effective in terms of the damage inflicted, but it was not decisive, since it could not prevent Togo from exercising sea control around the Liaodong Peninsula. The IJA General Staff's failure to create a decent siege train for Third Army was also a serious mistake, which led to very heavy casualties in the initial attacks on Port Arthur's outer defences. The purchase of even a few battalions of Krupp-made heavy guns in 1903, instead of after the war began, could have significantly reduced the duration of the siege. Nor did the IJA General Staff provide effective oversight of Nogi's botched attacks until it was clear that something was going seriously wrong at Port Arthur.

The performance of the front-line infantry during the Port Arthur campaign was remarkable and few armies could have stood up to this kind of strain for so long. Russian troops in Port Arthur were at their stoic best, never willingly surrendering a position despite suffering under a bombardment of nearly 17,000 28cm howitzer shells over a period of three months. On a typical day in November 1904, the Russian infantrymen on the crest of 203-metre Hill were being hit by the equivalent of 8 kilotons of high explosive, yet they held their smashed positions. In contrast, Belgian soldiers holding the Liège forts surrendered every position after just four days of shelling by German heavy siege howitzers in August 1914. Likewise, the Japanese infantry continued to show vigour in assault after assault, even after suffering 50 per cent casualties or more. Many Japanese troops did not expect to live to see victory at Port Arthur, and there were clearly moments of despair among the attackers. Neither side offered its troops any real respite for months, but simply more of the same each day – unlike the Western Front of 1915–18, where troops would be rotated to reserve positions after a week of front-line duty. In the end, the IJN – which had advocated vociferously for the Port Arthur campaign – came away without any tangible successes. The Russian Pacific Squadron had been eliminated by Nogi's Third Army at great cost, in order to gain a minor naval base which was of no further use to Japan. Nogi's siege cost the equivalent of three Japanese infantry divisions in order to eliminate two Russian infantry divisions – not a very good outcome for an economy of force operation. As for the Russians, they inflicted heavy casualties upon the enemy, but the exaggerated strategic value of Port Arthur made its capitulation a national catastrophe, which contributed to widespread internal unrest and revolt throughout the Russian Empire. The cost in lives, treasure and prestige expended at Port Arthur certainly did not represent a very favourable return for the ephemeral timber and mineral rights in Korea which had led to this outcome.

Russian wounded prisoners in Port Arthur after the surrender. The Japanese treatment of prisoners was exemplary and in accord with the Hague Convention of 1899. (Author's collection)

THE BATTLEFIELD TODAY

The house in Shuishiying where the surrender occurred is still preserved as a memorial. After the surrender, Nogi, Stoessel and their staffs dined together here. (Author's collection)

Port Arthur is now known as Lüshunkou District in the People's Republic of China. In the century since the Russo-Japanese War, the city's population has expanded more than twelve-fold and urban sprawl has covered up much of the battlefields of 1904. Unsurprisingly, the port of Lüshun is still an important naval base, but now hosting squadrons of Chinese destroyers, frigates, amphibious ships and submarines. Likewise, the simple dockyard of 1904 has been expanded into a major ship repair facility, which can accommodate and repair large warships. For a long time, Lüshun was closed to foreigners. Although the Liaodong Peninsula region has opened up in the past few decades, the military nature of Lüshun inveighs against tourism and most of the former Russian coast defences are located in off-limit areas. For example, the coastal battery positions on the Tiger Peninsula are still

extant, but not accessible. Instead, foreign tourists are encouraged to spend their time in the commercial port of Dalian (Dalny). China's COVID-19 lockdowns served to further isolate Lüshun from battlefield tourism.

With that proviso, Lüshun does have a number of extant locations of relevance to the Port Arthur campaign which can be visited by foreign tourists. Both Battery No. 13 (Golden Hill) and Battery No. 15 (Electric Cliff) still exist, although the batteries are now equipped with World War II-vintage naval artillery. There are some areas on the Wantai Heights which are accessible and relevant, particularly around the remains of Fort II. A memorial known as the 'East Jiguanshan fortress' is the only preserved site in China focused on the Russo-Japanese War. Visitors can walk right up to the surviving casemates – most in poor condition – as well as a Japanese cenotaph marking the location where General Kondratenko was killed. Some of the underground bunkers in Fort II can also be seen – testimony to the sturdy construction of the fortress. On the north-west corner of Lüshun, 203-metre Hill is now a nature park, with a monument completed in 1913, commemorating the Japanese soldiers who died seizing this position. The Chinese have also put up various historical panels, marking some of the key positions. When the Japanese occupied Port Arthur, they decided to build a monument to honour the Russian war dead, as well. The Russian military cemetery located south of Shuishiying was expanded during the Soviet administration of the port after World War II, but was then badly damaged during China's Cultural Revolution. In 2010, Russian President Dmitri Medvedev visited the cemetery, which was in the process of restoration. Rather surprisingly, an inscription in the cemetery's chapel reads: 'Here lie the mortal remains of the valiant Russian soldiers who fell defending the fortress of Port Arthur'.

A 6in. Canet gun mounted atop the remains of Fort II, now known as 'the North Fort of East Jiguanshan Fortress'. It is evident from this photo that the Russian guns on the Wantai Heights had excellent fields of fire, although clearly artillerymen could not survive for long in such exposed firing positions. (Author's collection)

FURTHER READING

Primary source records

Detailed Battle Report of the Siege Artillery Headquarters in the Lushun Area from August 25 to 31 1904, Ref: C13110506500. Japan Center for Asian Historical Records, National Archives of Japan.

Detailed Battle Report of Siege Artillery Headquarters in the Lushun Area from October 1st to October 10th 1904, Ref: C13110507000. Japan Center for Asian Historical Records, National Archives of Japan.

Official sources

The Official History of the Russo-Japanese War, Part III: *The Siege of Port Arthur*, Historical Section of the Committee of Imperial Defence (London: HMSO, 1909)

Secondary sources

Ashmead-Bartlett, Ellis, *Port Arthur: The Siege and Capitulation* (London: William Blackwood and Sons, 1906)

Biryuk, Sergey N., *Russkaya pekhota v Russko-yaponskoy voyne 1904–1905* (*Russian Infantry in the Russo-Japanese War 1904–1905*) (Moscow: Eksmo, 2021)

Connaughton, Richard, *Rising Sun and Tumbling Bear: Russia's War with Japan* (London: Cassell, 2003)

Drea, Edward J., *Japan's Imperial Army: Its Rise and Fall, 1853–1945* (Lawrence: University Press of Kansas, 2009)

Edgerton, Robert B., *Warriors of the Rising Sun: A History of the Japanese Military* (New York: W. W. Norton & Co., 1997)

Kersnovsky, A.A., *Istoriya Russkoy Armii* (*History of the Russian Army*), Vol. III (Moscow: Golos, 1994)

Ruckman, John W., 'The Command and Administration of the Fortress of Port Arthur During the Russo-Japanese War', *Journal of the United States Artillery*, Vol. 44, No. 3 (November–December 1915)

Tretyakov, Nikolai A., *My Experiences at Nan Shan and Port Arthur* (Uckfield: The Naval and Military Press Ltd, 2009)

Villiers, Frederic, *Port Arthur: Three Months with the Besiegers* (New York: Longmans, Green & Co., 1905)

Warner, Denis and Peggy, *The Tide at Sunrise: A History of the Russo-Japanese War 1904–1905* (New York: Charterhouse, 1974)

The remains of Fort II today, as a minor tourist attraction. The outer walls bear considerable shellfire damage, although it is clear that much of the structure survived the Japanese bombardments. (Author's collection)

INDEX

Figures in **bold** refer to illustrations.